· · · · · · · · · · · · · · · · · **FIRST-TIME
MOM**

OTHER RESOURCES BY
Dr. Kevin Leman

BOOKS

A Chicken's Guide to Talking Turkey with Your Kids about Sex
  (with Kathy Bell)
Sheet Music: Uncovering the Secrets of Sexual Intimacy
  in Marriage
Adolescence Isn't Terminal
The Real You: Become the Person You Were Meant to Be
Say Good-Bye to Stress
The Birth Order Connection
What a Difference a Daddy Makes
Making Children Mind without Losing Yours
Making Sense of the Men in Your Life
Becoming a Couple of Promise
Becoming the Parent God Wants You to Be
  (with Dave and Neta Jackson)
The Birth Order Book
Women Who Try Too Hard
When Your Best Is Not Good Enough
Bringing Up Kids without Tearing Them Down
Living in a Step-Family without Getting Stepped On
Unlocking the Secrets of Your Childhood Memories
  (with Randy Carlson)
Sex Begins in the Kitchen
10 Secrets for Raising Sensible, Successful Kids

VIDEO SERIES

Making Children Mind without Losing Yours—parenting edition
Making Children Mind without Losing Yours—public school
  edition for teachers, in-service sessions, PTA events
Bringing Peace & Harmony to the Blended Family
Single Parenting that WORKS! Raising Well-Balanced Children
  in an Off-Balance World
Making the Most of Marriage

First-Time Mom

Getting Off on the Right Foot—From Birth to First Grade

• • • • • • • • • • • • • • • • •

Dr. Kevin Leman

Tyndale House Publishers, Inc.
Wheaton, Illinois

Visit Tyndale's exciting Web site at www.tyndale.com

First-Time Mom

Copyright © 2004 by Kevin Leman. All rights reserved.

Cover photograph copyright © 2003 by Jimi Allen. All rights reserved.

Author photo copyright © 2002 by Tom Spitz Photography. All rights reserved.

Designed by Beth Sparkman

Edited by Ramona Cramer Tucker

Library of Congress Cataloging-in-Publication Data

Leman, Kevin.
  First-time mom : getting off on the right foot from infancy to first grade / Kevin Leman.
    p. cm.
Includes bibliographical references.
  ISBN 0-8423-6038-7 (hc) — ISBN 0-8423-6039-5 (pbk) — ISBN 0-8423-6040-9 (mass paper)
1. Child rearing. 2. Parenting. 3. Motherhood. I. Title.
HQ769.L375 2004
649′.1—dc22   2003020546

ISBN 0-8423-7383-7 (Int'l Edition)

Printed in the United States of America

09 08 07 06 05 04
7   6   5   4   3   2   1

For Conner—
You've got a great mom . . .
and dad too!

CONTENTS

ACKNOWLEDGMENT

*To the most competent,
encouraging, and wonderfully
gifted editor one could ask for—
Ramona Tucker*

*Ramona, the good guys at
Tyndale ought to pay you in
gold buillion. You're worth it.
Thanks for all your help.*

● ● ● ● ● ● ● ● ● ● ● ● ● ● ● ●

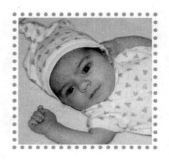

"I was born at a very young age."

—DR. LEMAN

"Babies are such a nice way to start people."[1]

—DON HEROLD

INTRODUCTION

The Adventure of a Lifetime

Welcome to the adventure of a lifetime!

If you're like most first-time moms, you're probably a little stunned to find out you're going to be a parent. You may be pregnant, soon to birth a child, or have recently birthed a child. You may be in the process of choosing a child through domestic or international adoption. Or you may recently have brought that child home. You may be married or single. But no matter how you've become a parent, as a first-time mom you have lots of questions, not to mention these biggies:

- How can I be the best mom for this child?
- Will this child be like me in any way? In personality, talents, or looks?
- Should I get her on a regular sleeping and eating schedule, or go with the flow?
- How do I know if he's getting what he needs to grow up healthy?
- What are some good ways to make sure I bond with this child—for a lifetime?
- How can I stop my child from crying so much? Am I doing something wrong?

- Will she go through those "terrible twos" of toddlerhood? I'm already starting to sweat.
- How should I handle discipline? Is spanking okay? At what age do kids understand discipline?
- Should we have just one child—or more?

And this is just the start of your questions. You could probably fill in a whole other page of your own additional ones. It's no wonder! Becoming a mom is a huge life transition,—one of constant surprises, joy, anxiety, sacrifices, and also tremendous rewards.

One of the reasons I've chosen to write this book is to help first-time mothers like you see that this thing called being a mom is actually a little easier than you might think. For thousands of years, parents have raised firstborns without any books, seminars, radio programs, or television specials telling them what to do, so take a deep breath. You won't be perfect, and your child won't be perfect. But together you will adjust to being a family, and you'll have a lot of laughter along the way.

This book will take you and your child from infancy through first grade (another time of transition where your child is away from you for a significant portion of the day). It will help you know what to expect as you bring your child home, what to focus on during the first ten days (when you and your child are so "new" to each other), and will help you relax as you realize that "The Big Three" (eating, sleeping, and crying) of your child's needs aren't as difficult as you might think. Then we'll journey on through the first year, talk about the ten most common first-time parenting mistakes. (Don't worry, we won't pick on you. Every parent on the planet makes a host of these mistakes. But you can be smart. Being aware of the mistakes is your best tool to building a healthy environment for your child to grow up in.)

We'll also talk about the issue of work. For those of you who already have careers and are used to working outside the home, we'll give you some things to think about in making your decision of whether or not to return to the workplace or to do work (other than raising your child, which is already a twenty-four-hour, seven-day-a-week job) from your home. I realize that for some of you, especially you single moms, the choice to work or not to work may not really be viable. In order to provide for your family, you will need to work. Let me assure you: The material in this chapter is not meant to be guilt-inducing but to give you practical information to help you make an informed decision that will be the best for you and your family in the long-term.

If you're married, you'll find chapter 7, "Caring for Your 'Other Child,'" helpful. No, we're not putting down guys (after all, I'm one myself), but the guy in your life may be going through more of a transition in becoming a father than you might think. I'll also reveal how your own firstborn, secondborn, and lastborn characteristics are affecting your and your spouse's parenting styles more than you might think.

Then, as your child grows, we'll plunge into "Toddler Time" and share the secret "Tricks of the Trade." Wonder when you should talk with your kids about sex? You can do it much earlier than you think, and still be age-appropriate (see chapter 11, "The Birds and the Bees"). And we'll even address other down-the-road questions you'll probably have: *Should I have another child? If so, will I love that child as much as I love my firstborn? And how will my firstborn handle a new sibling?*

You owe it to yourself—and your firstborn—to find out as much as you can about this new role of parenting and how babies work. So go ahead—plunge in!

1

Welcome Home

Good for you. You did it.

You're a parent! Maybe it happened through birth. Perhaps it was through adoption. But the agony of waiting through hours of labor or months of paperwork has finally culminated in you getting to meet your special treasure face-to-face. And now you're bringing that wonderful, incredible child home with you!

All sorts of emotions are flooding through you—a mixture of joy, wonder, and if you're smart, most likely a little healthy fear too. You wonder, *What kind of parent will I be? What will this child be like?*

If you birthed this child, you went to Lamaze class, wearing your sweats, carrying your pillows, and watching as your classmates' bellies bloated to ever-increasing proportions and then dropped with the weight of a bowling ball. You learned how to breathe in different patterns during those weekday-evening classes, while on the weekends you shopped in baby stores for your first crib, changing table, and baby clothes. You've scoured several books to find just the right name, insisting that no child of yours will ever be called Buford or Betty.

You suffered through months of restless, sleepless, and

seemingly eternal nights. You might have enjoyed the extra calories you could take in, but the sickness, nausea, backache, and swollen ankles you could have done without.

When the day finally came, you had five people in one small room, all telling you what to do. They all seemed so sure of themselves and, to be fair, encouraging of you. But it didn't take long for you to realize that you were the only one in the room who was in true pain.

Before you had the Epidural, you grabbed and clenched your fists, you thought words you never thought you would think, your throat was as dry as a desert, and all they would give you were those pitiful little ice chips, parceled out as if they cost a million dollars apiece—and yes, I know you were pushing as hard as you could. (I also happen to know that you wanted to punch out three or four people in the room.)

But as that special little gift from God worked her way down your birth canal and suddenly popped her head out, and those tiny shoulders worked their way through your body, you finally heard the delightful cry of your newborn. The doctor asked your husband if he'd like to cut the umbilical cord. A quick glance at your husband's queasy complexion told you he was in no shape to do anything.

And when that twenty-inch child was laid upon your breast, you buried your chin into your chest to get as good a look as possible at this new miracle, saying to yourself, *She's so beautiful. I can't believe she's mine.*

Or perhaps you became a parent through adoption. You spent months or years researching just the right people who could help you find "the child of your heart." You talked with multiple agencies, attorneys, agonized over how to become a parent, wondered *if* you would ever become a parent, investigated domestic and international routes, and, in hope, waded through enough paperwork to make you completely dizzy. If you had to travel internationally, you had doctor checkups too—and more painful shots than you want to remember.

Then all the feverish activity stopped, and the real waiting began. Even though you weren't physically pregnant, you were *emotionally* pregnant—waiting with longing for anywhere from months to years for your child. Perhaps you sat in a rocker, hand-stitching a baby blanket or dreaming your way through a baby-name book. Or perhaps you held off, worried that your heart would break if you didn't get a child. And then you got "the call" or "that first sweet picture." And you fell in love with that child from the first instant. Your world spun into the feverish activity. You did what you didn't dare to do before: bought a crib, decorated a baby's room, packed a bag with diapers, lotions, and all the essentials.

When you saw your child's face for the first time, you saw the realization of years of hopes, the joy after the pain of infertility or miscarriage. And your awe in holding that child was mixed with a pang of pain—knowing someone else's sacrifice to bring this child into your life. As you headed home, you vowed to be the absolute best parent you could be for this truly special child.

So, whether through birth or chosen through adoption, your firstborn has come into this life with a great entrée. Now the question is, what are you going to do with her?

WHAT HAVE WE DONE?

Remember: This isn't just an ordinary kid that you've brought home. She's a firstborn. It's not that subsequent children in your family will be chopped liver, but firstborns are a special breed (and, after all, the subject of this book!).

3

Although you may not be able to believe it looking at your tiny bundle of little toes and miniature fingers, nestled deep inside that baby blanket is a little Judge Judy or Judge Wapner.

Firstborns have a knack at excelling. You already know plenty of them. You've seen them in the movies or on television—Sharon Stone, Michelle Pfeiffer, Nicole Kidman, Sandra Bullock, Harrison Ford, Oprah Winfrey, Bill Cosby. They're all firstborns. You've read about them in your history books—George Washington, Jimmy Carter, Harry Truman, Bill Clinton, George W. Bush, and a whole host of other presidents. You've seen them excel in business (it seems that just about every CEO is a firstborn), and you've probably read some of their books—those of Dr. James Dobson (actually, since he's an only child, we'll call him a super firstborn!), Dr. D. James Kennedy, and William Shakespeare, to name just a few.

Firstborns are the generals of our world. Frequently exacting, very rule-conscious, normally conservative, your firstborn will probably be your most reliable child, if you have more than one child. The chances of him or her being an astronaut, engineer, or CPA are higher than you can imagine.

Despite your best efforts, this child will get more individual attention from you than any other children who might join your family down the road. For your part, you'll probably have higher expectations for this child than all of your other children combined (though I hope this book will challenge your thinking in that area). Why will all this be so? Think about it—this child is now your only child. She doesn't have to wait in front of the television while you fix dinner for another child. For one year, two years, three years, or maybe even four years (or a lifetime, if this firstborn is your only child), this baby will have you all to herself. Everything she does will be new to both of you. You'll clap for her first steps, coo over her first spit-up, and probably take pictures of her first bath. Her "baby book" will bulge with photographs, mementos, and keepsakes.

Down the road, if you do have more than one child, when the last child spits up, you'll probably either wait until bedtime to clean the shirt or ask your firstborn to grab a washcloth. When the middle child starts walking, you may mention it to your husband when he gets home from work, but other than that, you may think, *Yeah, it's about that time.* You'll probably buy a baby book for the middle child, but when he turns five you'll feel guilty for how empty and slim it is, compared to the firstborn's book.

Why is this? Because you've already seen everything a baby can do one, two, or three times before!

The extra attention a firstborn receives gives him a "performer's" mentality. He learns early on that he's there to meet expectations. This has the negative effect of creating some anxiety but the positive effect of making him really want to please you by being outstanding. Consequently, he'll wear responsibility and leadership like a pair of comfortable slippers.

So take heart—you've got an opportunity to raise a child who's a great leader and contributor. I've raised three firstborns, so I know what I'm talking about.

LIFE WITH A FIRSTBORN

"Now Dr. Leman," some of you might be saying, "how can anyone have *three* firstborns?"

Our true firstborn, Holly, came before all the other kids. Our second "firstborn," Kevin, was actually our third child, but as the first and only male he has taken on many firstborn characteristics. And our youngest surprise child, Lauren, is six years younger than her nearest sibling making her, in effect, a firstborn in many ways. After all, her siblings were all in school by the time she was born, so she has received from us all the extra attention a firstborn would receive.

They want to achieve.

Here's what life is like with a firstborn. I'll use Lauren as an example, since Holly is now thirty years old and out on her own.

Just after Easter break, I was taking Lauren, an extremely conscientious student, to her third-grade class. Lauren, believe it or not, was studying Latin. Even though as a psychologist I've spent a good bit of my life studying human nature, I have to confess that I never anticipated driving my eight-year-old daughter to school while she read Latin in the front seat.

Curious that Lauren was working so hard on the first day after a vacation, I asked, "Do you have a test in Latin today?"

"No," Lauren said, "I'm just reviewing my verbs."

As a lastborn, the only time I "reviewed" my verbs was when the neighborhood tough guy, Wooly Bully Wayne, used to teach me dirty words!

That's the positive side of a firstborn—they really do want to achieve. But that drive to achieve can have a negative side too. One semester Lauren's grades suddenly dropped from an A to a C. There's not a C thing I can think of about Lauren, so my wife, Sande, and I immediately went down to the school to see if we could find out what was going on.

As we sat down with Lauren's teacher, she explained that the big thing at Lauren's table was who gets done first. The first student to complete an assignment carries a great deal of clout in Lauren's peer group. Well, Lauren, by her nature, is not a hurry-up kind of a person. She can do A-level work, but not if she rushes. I remember several instances when Lauren would work on a homemade birthday card for three days or even a week; she doesn't just grind them out in five minutes like so many kids do. But a firstborn will usually rise to any challenge, particularly one that builds a sense of esteem and accomplishment, so Lauren sacrificed quality for speed—to become an integral part of a peer group.

They need to learn that failure is a part of life.

The normal firstborn wants to excel. Adding to this already inherent desire are overblown parental expectations—even more so because this is a first child. Many parents today attempt to build their own self-esteem by pushing their children to excel at everything. They view second place as losing out to first place, rather than being well above average, which is quite wonderful in itself. Firstborns quickly pick up this mentality and run with it; they are the family's flag bearers.

7
* * * * *

However, as you'll see later, I believe the home ought to be a place where kids learn to fail, because failure is a part of life. It isn't something to be feared; it's something you learn from. And then you pick yourself up and go on. But you'll probably have a harder time putting that philosophy into practice with your firstborn than you will with any later children.

They are examples for later (if any) siblings.

There's yet another element that makes firstborns so different from later children. Because your firstborn is older, his younger siblings will look up to him with awe. As the baby of my family, I wanted to do everything my older brother did. He was my biggest hero, and I wanted to be just like him.

The oldest-born child is usually the strongest, smartest, and biggest in the family. If he has several younger siblings, by the time they catch up to him, he's already moved out of the house!

That's all the more reason to raise your firstborn right. If your younger children look up to him, you want him to set a good example. Though it's likely that at least one of the younger siblings will eventually rebel against his example, you still want the example to be there.

Even though I tell first-time parents all this information in my seminars and counseling practice, many still fall into the first-time-parent syndrome. And so will you. My wife, Sande, and I did too. You probably *will* expect too much from your firstborn. You will be stricter with him than with any of your other children. You will follow his progress more closely than all of your other children combined. More likely than not, however, this child will ultimately reward you for that attention.

GET READY FOR THE TINY TYRANT!

Two months ago, it was just you, if you're a single parent, or you and your husband, if you're married.

If you're a single parent, you're used to making decisions on your own—getting advice from others and then making the final call. If you're married, formally or informally, you two have worked out a compromise for who has what kind of power and influence in your family decisions. Like most couples, you've probably grown fairly comfortable with this arrangement. The lines have been drawn, both of you understand how it works, and you've reached a relative state of peace.

All that is about to change.

She'll take over your life.

This child, as innocent as she seems, and as docile as she appears, will immediately begin to formulate a game plan to completely take over your life, your home, your checkbook, and every second of your day. I'm not kidding you, and I'm not exaggerating. It's human nature. Your child is going to figure out how to manipulate you. Consciously or unconsciously, she's going to explore what buttons need to be pushed in order to get you to do what she wants you to do.

Are you motivated by fear? She'll learn to prey on that. Do you give in to relentless whining? She'll figure that one out soon enough. Are you persuaded by hostile rebellion? If so, she'll be all over you.

She'll have a strong sense of order.

You'll always have a power struggle with this child. By nature, first children tend to be a very meticulous breed. Holly wouldn't accept it when I told her, "Oh, honey, we'll be leaving around nine o'clock." If I tried that, she'd say, "But how long after nine o'clock? Or are we leaving before nine o'clock? What do you mean 'around nine o'clock?'"

I had to learn to say, "Holly, we're going to leave at 9:05."

And at 9:06, I'd get a firm reminder: "Dad, we're running late!"

Firstborns have a need for order. They like to be in charge, and for good reason: They usually are!

She'll lead the pack and figure everything out.

It's like this. I have a friend who runs road races and marathons. I tried to point out to him once that the marathon got its name from a 26.2 mile run accomplished by a messenger who delivered the news and then promptly died, but my friend didn't get the hint. Because he's an accomplished runner, he has to do something that the vast majority of people who enter races don't worry about: He has to know the course. When there's a good possibility you'll be leading the race, you can't just follow the pack. The vast majority of runners can show up ten minutes before the start, knowing there will always be people in front that they can follow to the course's end.

My marathoner friend's need to know the course is the family role of the firstborn. They are going to be in semicharge of any younger siblings for their entire lives. When you bring home baby number two, three, four, or even (don't gasp, we haven't reached my number yet!) five, each one of those kids can look around them to see what's expected of them and to determine how things are run. Your firstborn will never have that. With the later children, the firstborn is proudly thinking to herself, *Been there, done that. I know this house. I know these parents. I've got everything figured out.* You don't have to give them the role of person in charge; they'll just assume it!

Because they operate with the notion that they're in charge, firstborns tend to be more stubborn. Though Sande and I still can't figure out how Holly did it, one time she managed to somehow "pole vault" over the top of her crib when we were a few minutes behind schedule in getting her up.

But Lauren, our youngest child, would have happily stayed in her crib till she was five years old! Lauren was born in August. We spend the summers in New York state, so Lauren's first "bedroom" was a walk-in closet, about twelve feet by eight feet. She loved it in there. In the morning we'd catch her talking to herself, singing and making noises, as contented and happy a baby as you would ever find. If we came back an hour and a half later, she'd still be keeping herself pleasantly occupied.

Now, if we had tried that with Holly Leman—leaving her in a closet for an hour or more—our firstborn would have had the hinges off the door within five minutes and figured out how to call the police within ten. I'd be writing this book in jail, because Holly would find the best lawyer in town.

THERE'S A FIRST TIME FOR EVERYONE

By now some of you may be asking skeptically, "Are first-borns and middleborns and lastborns really all *that* different?"

The answer is, "More than you'll ever be able to believe." For starters, keep in mind that your firstborn baby has just as much experience being a baby as you have being a mom! When the secondborn rolls around, you'll have been a mom for a good eighteen to thirty-six months (or more). But this first child has you matched from the moment he arrives.

That allows him to play some fun "games." Holly was a master at this. When she was thirsty, if I brought her water from the bathroom, she insisted that she wanted kitchen water; if I brought kitchen water, Holly of course wanted bathroom water.

You think I made that mistake with Krissy (our second child)? Not a chance! Krissy never knew where the water came from. By the time child number two came around, I had learned not to overexplain things or to set myself up for another power struggle.

But please don't look at these firstborn characteristics as a negative; many positive qualities come from them. As I already mentioned, the overwhelming number of society's leaders, government officials, CEOs, and professionals are

11

* * * * *

firstborns. Your first child will probably amaze you with her spunk.

I remember when Holly decided to withdraw herself from preschool. She had enjoyed the first few months until some politically correct educators decided to transform what had been a good school into an "experimental learning center." It didn't take long for Holly to get fed up with this nonsense. One night she matter-of-factly announced that she wasn't going to go to school anymore.

"Honey, you have to go to preschool," I said.

"But I don't like the preschool anymore," Holly answered.

What Holly didn't realize is that her mom and I had already had some serious discussions about our growing concerns with the school. Just for fun, however, I decided to continue this conversation with Holly to see where she would go with it.

"Holly, if you aren't going back to preschool, you have to call them and let them know. You can't just stop showing up." Keep in mind—Holly was just three years old at the time.

"But Daddy," Holly said, "I don't know their phone number."

I, as Holly's doctor-degreed dad, wasn't about to give in to a three-year-old. So with my vast amounts of training and study, I figured I'd call her bluff. I gave Holly the phone number, deciding to force the issue.

Well, I soon learned that you don't force the issue with a kid like Holly. She actually called the school! At three years old!

"Hello? This is Holly Leman, and I'm not coming to school no more."

Take that, school! I'm in charge! That was exactly what she was saying. And that left me, as her dad, with a lot of explaining to do.

It all goes to show that you need to be prepared to raise this first child. Firstborns are challenging, but in many ways I envy what you have in store for you. I have thoroughly enjoyed Holly, as well as the other two children in my family who share some firstborn characteristics. Firstborns are challenging, but they are also bright, exceptional children. They can be a great joy!

ME? CHANGE THE WORLD?

The truth is, if you raise this first child right, you're going to change the world. And that's not an overstatement. The confidence of being a firstborn, coupled with a positive parenting experience, will usually result in a child who makes the world a much different place. She might be a teacher, a CEO, a very responsible parent, or president of the United States—but you can bet she's going to accomplish something. Firstborns are far more likely to be successful, to gain financial independence, and even to look after you in your old age.

13
* * * * *

After a few months of having this child in your home, you may be tempted to go back to "life as normal," trying to hold on to how things were before this child arrived. Please don't. Invest all you can into this child. Give her the love she needs, the time she deserves, and do all you can to "be there" for her. Your decision to become a parent means that you'll need to make some sacrifices in order to assume the added responsibility of a child. But please know that raising this child will be the most influential thing you can ever accomplish—and a true gift that can change the world around you in ways you never dreamed.

You have a great adventure ahead of you!

2

The First Ten Days

Your game plan for the first ten days with your child is a
simple one: survival.

If you've birthed this child, your body has just gone
through an ordeal that would make the Boston Marathon or
the Tour de France seem like a hop, skip, and a jump. Not
only were you tired out from being nine months pregnant,
you then went through the long ordeal of actually giving
birth. At the hospital, people came by to see your baby and
brought gifts and flowers. You tried to make yourself as
presentable as possible to accommodate the well-meaning
visitors when all you wanted to do was sleep.

Now, suddenly, you're sent out of the hospital with a
small bag of diapers and a baby. And you feel overwhelmed.
Not only are you recovering from your little special gift's
great voyage down the mighty Mississippi (also known as the
birth canal), but you're feeling the pressure to be the best
mommy you can possibly be. You love this baby so intensely,
and yet you're exhausted and more than a little scared.

If you've chosen this child, you may have received a
newborn, a toddler, or even an older child. You may have
met your child at a local hospital right after birth, driven to a
nearby town, or flown thousands of miles. You're so excited

emotionally—after going through all the reams of paperwork, your dreams are about to become true. Finally you're going to get to meet your child. You've spent months or years wondering what she'll look like. And now, suddenly, you're a little scared. As a first-time parent of a young child, you're trying to learn the new language of sippy cups, pacifiers, burp cloths (who would think of owning *one* of these, much less several?), car seats, strollers. You have happily pushed your "dry clean only" clothes to the back of your closet. You have spent days in baby stores, trying to guess the size of your new family member and translate the mystery of the suggested "pounds" on the tags onto a real body shape and size. If you've flown internationally, you're also physically exhausted. Your child is used to one time zone; you're in an entirely different one. Your day is her night; her night is your day.

And when you arrive home you're immediately surrounded by well-meaning visitors, who are all thrilled for you and want to see this child. You had thought you'd be so excited about showing her off. Now all you want to do is "cocoon" yourself, snuggle this child who is finally in your arms, and sleep.

Questions swirl in your mind: *Will I be a good parent? Will I give her what she needs to thrive physically, emotionally, and spiritually? Will she and I be able to bond quickly? In what ways will she be like me? Will she have my love for music? my sense of humor?*

TAKE A DEEP BREATH

Whether you've received this gift through birth or adoption, here's a suggestion: Just for these first ten days, concentrate on being a *good* mommy, as opposed to the *best* mommy. Let's be honest: You're not at your best. You're tired, you're sore, you're swimming in emotions, and if you just gave birth, your hormones are going bonkers. When first-time moms put too much pressure on themselves—*I'm going to be the best mom who has ever lived!*—they set themselves up for guilt and feelings of failure. And who needs that?

So get your breath back. Parenting is about decades, not days. You're going to face exhaustion and stress for the immediate future (well, okay, for the next twenty or so years, until your child is out of the nest and on her own!), so if you don't take care of yourself, you're going to burn out. Taking a semi-breather for ten days won't damage your child's intellectual development, social adjustment, or personal esteem. Forget about all the "shoulds" of parenting, and just take time to rest and bond.

17

In other words, you don't have to get any work done. There—feel better already? Let me say it plainly: I don't care if the house gets a little dirty. I don't care if the laundry piles up. I don't care if you aren't doing "brain developing" exercises with your baby. I want you to rest, relax, enjoy your new child, and bond as a family. I want you to get as much sleep as you can, which means that most of you will have to learn to sleep when your child sleeps.

In fact, let me give you Dr. Leman's prescription: When the baby lies down, don't turn into a tornado, scrubbing the floors and trying to make things perfect. Instead, focus on energizing your own body. Take the time to rest as well. You should take lots of little catnaps.

Oh, you'll be tempted to catch up on the laundry or clean the floors when your little angel takes her nap, but resist the temptation. Take a nap yourself. If you feel truly rested, give yourself permission to have a nice deluxe cup of coffee while reading a novel or magazine. Give yourself time to recover—you've been through a lot, and you have a long road ahead.

But it's not an impossible road to travel, as you may sometimes feel when you're exhausted and overwhelmed. And you know what? Parenting can be a lot of fun and very rewarding, too.

THE PRESSURE'S OFF!

Parents of first children tend to overdo things. They read all the parenting and "what to expect" books, do incredible amounts of research, scour stores for products their child "just has to have," and talk with any other parents within miles about their experiences. They have the Mozart and Shakespeare tapes for baby's brain development; antibacterial soap for anyone who touches anything that baby might touch; two thousand dollars' worth of special safety-first playpens, changing tables, and cribs; toys that have been tested, approved, and given a most vigorous inspection; and a ten-step diaper-change program, with organic cleaner, germ-destroying rinse, hypoallergenic powder to prevent diaper rash, and who knows how many ointments—all to keep baby's bottom in working order.

But let me tell you something: Your baby's bottom is a pretty durable instrument. Sure, for the sake of hygiene you want to clean it up now and then, but God didn't design something that will break down in fifty diaper changes without five hundred dollars' worth of special ointments, oils, and powders to keep it in working order!

For a baby's first few days of life, just take care of the basics: Your baby will sleep, your baby will eat, your baby will sleep some more, your baby will go potty, and your baby will go back to sleep. All these things are the most natural acts in the world for a baby to do. And guess what? You don't have to orchestrate any of them! They are, quite thankfully, very natural happenings.

So don't make the simple confusing. When the baby is wet, change him. If you forget, he'll probably remind you—and loudly. If you have an unusually compliant baby and he doesn't remind you and his bottom gets a little rash, there are ointments that will take care of it. Your child won't be scarred for life by having a bit of a diaper rash now and then (besides, who's going to check when he reaches high school?).

In other words, the pressure's off. The most important biological things that your baby needs to do—eat, sleep, and go potty—will happen quite naturally. Parents from previous centuries had none of the luxuries we have today, and even less of the knowledge. They didn't have antibacterial soap; they didn't have disposable diapers, or even hot water in many cases. They didn't have bottles with special nipples designed to fit a child's growing teeth without harming them. Yet in spite of all they didn't have, their babies not only survived, but also thrived.

You may think you don't know much, but I bet you know more than most moms have known from previous centuries. And the good news is that within just a few days, you're going to become a little expert, and you'll get good at understanding your little son or daughter. In fact, you'll understand your baby better than anyone else in the world. You'll know what your baby needs just by the sound of her cry. You'll be able to read her better than anyone else can, including your doctor.

TAILOR-MADE BONDING

You only get one chance to welcome your child into this world and into your home, so make the most of it. A child won't understand if you put a premium on a clean house, a certain style of meal preparation, ironed clothes, or television watching. The only thing baby knows is that he wants to be with you—and he will get fussy if you're too busy or distracted by other things.

I've already mentioned that the three most important biological acts—eating, sleeping, and going potty—will happen naturally, but there's another very important relational act. It's called bonding. This is a time for you and your child to get physically, spiritually, and emotionally connected.

20
• • • • •

Get close, skin to skin.

One of the most powerful bonding exercises between a mother and baby is one designed by God himself: breast-feeding. There isn't a warmer or more comfortable place on earth for a baby than to be tucked against mommy's stomach, nestled to her breasts. And the food is free! (Something you certainly won't be able to say later in the child's life, especially in the hungry adolescent and teenage years.)

If you have birthed this child, I hope you'll take advantage of this wonderful bonding opportunity. If you aren't able to breast-feed for some reason, or if your child is chosen, don't despair. You can still make bottle-feeding a slow, unhurried, and intimate experience. Pull up your shirt so baby can get some skin time. Nothing feels as good as skin—not even premier cotton with a GAP, Oshkosh, or Ralph Lauren label. Look into your baby's eyes; sing to her, talk to her, laugh with her (children love to hear you laugh). Avoid the trap of seeing nursing or feeding time as a way to watch television, talk on the phone, or do something else without any "vocal" interruptions. Use baby's naptime for these diversions.

"Wear" your baby!

Another great opportunity to bond is easier today than ever before: Keep your baby with you as much as possible. Back in my day kids were often placed in mobile pens or infant seats where they were separated from you. Today, fortunately, there are any number of baby carriers that allow you to virtually "wear" your baby. These are great ideas. I've seen some that allow baby to rest, sitting up, against your chest, and others that allow baby to lie down in an elaborate sling. As baby grows a bit, you can get backpacks for your walks. If you've chosen an "older baby" or a toddler, set aside a lot of time for snuggling. Carry that child next to your heart as much as you can and do a lot of rocking with the child on your lap. Any investment you make in keeping your child close to you will pay infinite rewards in emotional and physical bonding.

When you purchase a stroller, consider getting one that allows you to look at your baby, instead of one that has your baby pointing away from you. If you can afford it, perhaps you can purchase one of each. Your child will grow familiar with the world soon enough; in the early months she's as interested in you as anything she'll see out on the street.

Maximize night and morning times.

There are two other times tailor-made for bonding: just as your child wakes up in the morning, and as she goes to sleep at night. Think about it—what would you dream about most often if you saw the same face smiling down at you every night, just before you dropped off to sleep, and then greeting you first thing in the morning? Such consistency provides a firm foundation of safety for your child.

I'm not a medical doctor, but my counselor's training gives

me some authority to speak on this: Psychologically, your child will greatly benefit from unhurried bonding time, particularly before bedtime. Some children are also eager to cuddle right after they wake up. There really is no substitute, no amount of "quality time," that can replace these ideal windows.

Fall in love.

Bonding isn't a complicated process; it's natural. Every time you talk and interact with your baby, you bond. You're falling in love with your baby—and your baby is falling in love with you. Giving her a little raspberry on her tummy, touching her toes and talking to her while you change her diaper, singing softly as she slips into sleep—these are all precious times of bonding together.

Resist the "hurry trap."

Even now your child is constantly looking up and taking emotional notes on how he or she is treated. So resist the traditional hurried American lifestyle. Children are very sensitive to getting the brush-off; they have a way of knowing what's going on when you're just trying to get them to take a nap prematurely because you have other things to do.

"But Dr. Leman," some of you may be asking, "what's premature? How long should I wait until I put my baby down for another nap?"

There's a reason this book isn't filled with a lot of charts. I am a big proponent of letting your child be the unique being that she is. Ask any young mom in a MOPS (Mothers of Preschoolers) group who has a couple of kids, and she'll tell you that every kid is different. Is there a time that's best to put your child down for a nap or bedtime? Absolutely. What time is that? It depends on your child!

This is why bonding is so crucial. When you get to know your child, she will give you cues to show you when she's sleepy. Some babies will rub their eyes, others will start to fuss every time they are moved or touched, others will scream bloody murder. As you get to know your baby, you'll learn to pick up on these cues before you have a major confrontation. The better you know your baby, the better you'll be at timing those important events like eating and sleeping. Anticipating these moments will take some of the steam out of the power struggles that will arise in the coming months.

There's no substitute for time. You've got to take the time to learn how to read your child. Everything else—like dishes stacked high, dust bunnies in the corners, returning phone calls and e-mails—can wait.

23
• • • • •

THE NOISE FACTOR

What's the first thing you do when you bring a child home for the first time and she falls asleep? "Shh!" you say, finger to lips. "Let her sleep." So you lay her gently in her crib, tuck a blanket around her, and then back out of the room, closing the door quietly. Then you spend the rest of her nap tiptoeing around so you don't make a sound. Even when she's awake, you fear startling her with any noise.

Most first-time mothers and fathers, I've found, treat their newborn just like that—as if the child is a pheasant under glass. They *ooh*, they *ahh*, and their house becomes as silent as a tomb. They wince when the doorbell sounds or the phone rings. They hesitate to even put dishes away since it might "wake up the baby."

However, all babies need to get used to "normal household" noise. That means you, as parent, should go about your normal tasks. Treat the noise that goes along with those tasks as beneficial: "Mommy needs to vacuum the floor right now because it's really messy and it needs to be cleaned. The vacuum cleaner makes a funny buzzing sound. Want to hear it?" Then turn on the vacuum cleaner and show what it does. You can even follow up with, "When you're older, you can even help me. What a treat that will be!" Of course a newborn won't necessarily understand this conversation, but the very tone of your voice—happy, pleasant—will convey crucial information to your child about noise. Children need to learn that noise isn't something to be feared; it's a part of life. Every child will hear the clinking of dishes, the whirr of a vacuum cleaner, the boom of thunder, the crackling of lightning—and if you portray all these as a normal part of life, a child will attach no fear to such noises.

A mom who had two toddlers put this "noise factor" to good use. When the toddlers decided to have a shouting match in the car, to see which one could be louder (and they were at the age where they didn't know how loud they really were), she turned on the radio so loud that the toddlers covered their ears.

"Mom! It's too loud," they said in unison.

Smiling, she turned down the radio. Then she wisely said, "Well, that's exactly what your shouting match sounds like to me. Too loud."

The toddlers looked at each other with arched eyebrows and said, "Then we'll talk in our *regular* voices."

Children are smart. They get the point. And they also understand what you are *not* saying by watching your reactions.

So don't tiptoe around your house, afraid of making noise. Noise is a part of your home, a part of daily life. Does this mean you should go around purposely banging a toy drum next to your child's ears? Of course not. But the sooner a child gets used to noise, the easier her adjustment into your home life will be.

AN ASSIGNMENT FOR ALL PARENTS

You've got your hands full these first ten days, but I want to give you one additional—and very important— assignment. Somewhere in the first two weeks of your child being home with you, I want you to go out for dinner with your husband, leaving the baby at home. If you're a single parent, it's important for you to take some time with friends, too—away from your child.

25
• • • • •

For some of you, this may be the hardest thing a doctor has ever asked you to do. After all, you may have waited and longed for years for this child. Now that she's in your home you want to stay close by, in order to protect her and bond with her. You want her to feel your love constantly surrounding her. But it's also vital for your own well-being, the long-term health of your family, and ultimately for your child's lifelong welfare for you to take some time away. For starters, it sets the guideline that mom isn't always going to be there; your child needs to learn that you do have a life outside of him.

Secondly, if you're married, going out on a date early on with your husband reinforces the importance of the two of you continuing to work on your relationship. One of the best things you can do for your child is to make a commitment to make your marriage work. Do you want your baby to grow up in a marriage where Mom and Dad are virtual strangers to each other? Do you want your baby to grow up and think that Mom and Dad only tolerate each other, at best? Or do you want your child to model her own marriage relationship after the one she witnessed at home, one day saying to herself, *I hope my marriage is as good and rich and meaningful as my parents?*

But I already know the excuse you're going to use to get out of this assignment because I've heard it numerous times before: "There's no one 'qualified' to watch the baby." Of course your first instinct is that you have to have someone with a Ph.D. in medical nursing and a graduate degree in infant psychology to boot. But just about any responsible adult can take care of a baby for two or three hours, and that's all I'm asking you to give up. No, you don't want to leave a young baby with someone who is just getting started in baby-sitting—this is not the time to try out thirteen- or fourteen-year-olds—but a mature adult, whether it be an aunt, a grandma, a grandpa, or a caring neighbor, will do just fine. If you time it right, the baby might be sleeping most of that time anyway.

For married couples, part of your assignment is to begin your date with the statement "Let's talk about us." At first this might be hard to do—but you absolutely must continue to build your life as a couple. Two great challenges I've seen to marital romance occur just after the wedding and just after the first baby comes home. Why? Some engaged couples quit talking about each other and spend all their time planning the wedding. Then, once the wedding is over, they don't have anything to talk about! And rookie parents often get lost in their children, slowly becoming strangers to each other. They talk about the nursery, the upcoming delivery or the adoption dossier, how things went at the hospital, what baby did for the first time today. There's a reason we counselors only half-jokingly refer to "the idolatry of the firstborn."

Those of you who think you can't possibly leave your

baby or that you certainly can't *not* talk about your baby while away on a date need a little advice from someone who has been there. Trust me on this one. Three years from now, you and your husband—if you're wise—will arrange to get away for an entire weekend. As Friday approaches, you'll be as giddy as little kids. Though your heartstrings will be tugged a bit as you drive off leaving little Betty or Buford behind (if you're saying right now, *Hey, I thought you said earlier in the book that you'd never call your kids that,* congratulations—you're a careful reader!*)*, you'll say things like, "I can't believe we're going to be alone for three whole days."

And when you arrive at the restaurant, you'll give each other knowing looks, maybe play footsy under the table, and enjoy a leisurely dinner without having to cut someone else's food into bite-size chunks. For the first time in months, you'll be able to have sex before 9:00 P.M., without worrying that someone in the house may hear what you're doing.

27

Of course, after your little romantic interlude, you'll eventually look at the clock and say, "I wonder if Betty is okay . . . think we should call home?"

The truth is, you'll never get too far away from your kids, at least emotionally—they suck us into their lives even if several hundred miles separate us—but that shouldn't stop you from working hard to reserve time for your marriage. By the end of the wonderful weekend, if the truth is known, you'll hardly be able to wait to get your hands on that little guy and to see that happy, goofy grin. Your heart will almost be overwhelmed at how much you missed him. That's the nature of being a parent: finding your heart intertwined with that of your child's. And that's especially why it's so important, from the very start, to set the precedent of spending time alone together as a couple.

Remember what I said earlier: Parenting is about decades, not days. It is dangerous to your family's welfare to put your marriage on hiatus while you try to raise a child. One of the worst things that can happen to a child psychologically is to go through her parents' painful divorce. So you're doing your baby a favor by leaving her long enough to attend to your marital needs.

EVERYTHING CHANGES

Most of us know the feeling of driving down the highway, seeing brake lights suddenly appear in front of us, slamming

on the brakes, and missing the car in front of us by inches. That's an immediate, short-term kind of stress that all of us face from time to time, and our body is well-equipped to handle the sudden surge of adrenaline. Twenty minutes later, our body is back to a state of normalcy. That's not the kind of stress that *will* do long-term damage to your body.

Ironically, the kind of stress that will kill you is the slow, pervasive, unremitting kind—the neighbor's dog that won't stop barking and that keeps you up night after night; feelings of continued powerlessness at work, where you always have more work to get done than time to do it; ongoing resentment about a personal relationship. These aren't as intense as the almost-getting-in-an-accident kind of panic, and they don't raise your heartbeat quite as high, but the stress produced by these ongoing frustrations is very real—and even more damaging to our body's systems.

Now, what kind of stress do you think is more likely to rear its head in parenting? That's right, the more deadly kind.

Here's the problem: If you as a woman are anything like Sande Leman (my wife), you can shop for hours on end. You can shop all day. In fact, wearing the right pair of shoes, and given enough coffee and an occasional dose of chocolate, you can shop for an entire weekend. But will your car battery last that long if you leave the lights on?

Absolutely not. If you leave your headlights burning, no matter what kind of a "Diehard" you have, your car battery is going to run out somewhere between leaving Nordstrom and entering Sears.

It's the same with being the mother of a young child. You can only take so much. Forget what you were able to get done before you had a child. Every word must take on a new definition. For instance, the words *clean, schedule,* and *gourmet cooking* will all have to be redefined in the first few months of your new baby's life. In time, a "clean" house will mean there are places where you can actually see the floor. For some of you, this won't be hard; for others of you, it's going to be a real stretch to learn how to lower your expectations.

Here's why I think it's so important that you do lower your expectations. Your little gift from God could care less about your housework, your need for sleep, or your need to work out at the club with your friend. You have been given a gift but, to put it bluntly, he is a hedonistic little sucker. All that baby cares about is to be warm, comfortable, cuddled, talked-to, fed, and rested.

If you try to do everything you did before you had a baby, you may grow resentful toward your child. The problem is not your child—she's acting like all children act! The problem is your belief that bringing a child home won't appreciably change your schedule, your housecleaning, or your ability to cook, relax, and play. In the first ten days, I want you to bond with your child, not grow angry or resentful toward your child. This is your time to let the rest of the

29

world run on its own while you simply focus on getting to know each other.

Isn't it amazing that in these first few days of life, a little almost twenty-incher learns to recognize who you are? She can identify your distinctive, loving voice. If your new child is an older baby or toddler, soon he will be comforted by the soothing sound of your voice and the circle of your arms. No one can take your place in his heart. Whether a "chosen" or birthed child, you are, no doubt, going to fall in love with each other.

But these are just the first few steps of the long journey of parenthood. If your child lives with you for eighteen years (and many children will be with you longer than that), you're going to have over 6,500 days to raise your child. The first ten days are literally the first step. No wise runner starts sprinting at the start of a marathon, so pace yourself.

Here's an analogy I like to use. If you have ever traveled on an airplane, you know the announcement given at the start of the flight. In the event of an emergency, parents who are flying with young children are urged to put on their own masks before they secure a mask on their child. Why? If you pass out putting on your kid's mask, both of you are in trouble.

In the adventure of parenting, you need your own oxygen before you will be physically and spiritually strong enough to care for someone else. In the first ten days, bonding with your child will be a full-time, around-the-clock responsibility. Housework, fancy meals, visitors, and sometimes even showering may have to wait. Keep first things first and your priorities straight. Any household runs best if the focus is on God first (where else can you get renewed strength when you feel exhausted except through prayer and God's gift of sleep?), your husband second (if you are married), and your child third. But when your child is young, it's easy to put the third in the first position. Sande and I know—we've had to work hard over the last thirty years of parenting (we now have a span from a thirty-year-old child to a ten-year-old child) to keep our own priorities straight.

Also, keep things simple. Some of you moms have already read half a dozen books on parenting. While I applaud your industry, I want to caution you about overdoing it. Too much information can be very confusing.

Put it this way: Have you ever been in a group and asked out loud for someone to give you the time so you could reset your watch? Remember all the conflicting answers you got?

"9:45."

"9:55."

"9:43."

"9:47."

If you're trying to set your own watch, and you only need to know what time it is, getting several answers can be more confusing than even getting one slightly wrong answer. Parenting is kind of like that. You're better off wearing one watch, and your child will be better off with you following one simple game plan. Consistency is probably more important than just about anything else.

The most consistent and simple formula I can give you for the first ten days is to bond and to recover. *Bond and recover.* Spend time with your child. Rest. Laugh with your baby. Rest. Feed your baby. Rest. Change your baby's diaper. Rest.

Every day your child is going to become a little bit more independent. She'll need you a little less. Enjoy these days when you are your baby's entire world. It's a sacred time, and you've earned it.

A SPECIAL WORD FOR THE FIRST-TIME DAD

Most of this book will be read by you, the mother. But if you're married, I want to ask you to bookmark this section and have your husband read it.

Dad, this is just for you. I know, I know—you've got a hundred things to do around the house, and about a dozen games you want to watch on television, so you're not too thrilled that your wife has handed you this book and asked you to read this section. I'll make it as brief as I can (hey, it takes a guy to know another guy's attention span!), but I do believe that what I'm about to say is pretty impor-tant.

Your wife has just been part of a great miracle. Yeah, I know, you were part of it, too, if you conceived this child together. But your part was a little more fun than her part, and her part lasted nine months (if you're lucky, your part lasted an hour and a half; on average, I'd say it probably lasted about fifteen minutes!).

Let me talk to you dad to dad—yeah, you're a dad now. You might still feel like a kid or like you're much too young to actually have a child call you "Dad," but the child that just came out of your wife's body certainly qualifies you for that distinction.

I've raised five kids of my own, and if I can do it, you can too. I know how to play possum—keeping a very steady sleep-sounding rhythm going in my breathing so my wife wouldn't even think about "waking" me to ask me to help clean up a dirty diaper or a sick kid's vomit. In fact, after five children, I think it's safe to say that I know every trick of the trade.

But I've also, thankfully, done my share of helping. After thirty years of childrearing, Sande would tell you I've been a pretty good dad. Sande appreciates that I've been willing to roll up my sleeves and help, and that's what I want to talk to you about.

Realize you're the "ace reliever"!

Right now your wife is an all-star. In baseball terms, she's Roger Clemens. She's been asked to throw the heat for eight straight innings and it's been a tough game. As much as Roger doesn't want to come out of the ball game, the number of pitches he's thrown and his exhaustion dictate that he has to come out. When Joe Torre walks onto the field, Roger knows his time is up; now the game lies in the hands of Mariano Rivera, the ace reliever.

If your wife is Roger Clemens, you're Mariano Rivera. You may never have seen yourself as Rivera, but you are; you're the reliever. Your wife may not want to get off the mound, but for the sake of her health and your baby and ultimately your own happiness, you have to protect her from overdoing it.

As the reliever, your job is to roll up your sleeves and finish what your wife started. If your baby takes short naps, your wife may need to sleep while you watch junior. Certainly she could use the ten minutes to relax on the couch while you change a diaper. Giving her these minivacations several times a day (even if it means right when you walk in the door from work and she's looking frazzled, in the middle of the night, or early in the morning before work) will make all the difference in the world for you, your wife, and your child.

I know, I know—you've been working all day, too. Sure, you'd like to come home, read the paper, and catch up on the scores. But your work is different; at least you've been able to change locations and the type of work. Contrast that to your wife, whose entire day has been wrapped up in caring for your child. She is feeling a tremendous daily, minute-by-minute responsibility for a child who is not yet capable of doing things for himself. Whether she worked outside the home before or not, becoming a mom has changed her entire world. She needs a break.

Frankly, your wife's energy, previously poured into you and your marriage, has now been severely disrupted by this twenty-inch gift from God, whom you may have noticed has many hedonistic tendencies and can't give back to her at all. That's why she needs your help. Her number one obstacle will always be exhaustion. Think of her as a driver being pulled out of the car after an Indy 500—so stiff and sore she can barely stand. That's your wife. Physically, emotionally, hormonally, she's been involved in a war. And at times she needs you to carry the load for a while.

Be your wife's hero.

Being a mom of a young child is really difficult. It's a twenty-four-hour-a-day job. No wonder so many moms decide to stay home with their children (more on this in a later chapter). And yet some people look down on stay-at-home moms, figuring that they're not contributing much to society. Those misguided people have a lot to learn about the challenges of being a mother who's "on call" around the clock. And so does any father who works outside the home and doesn't see the minute-by-minute challenges his wife faces. But you can be different. You have the opportunity to be your wife's hero and a great father to your child by stepping up to that pitching mound and taking the ball from your wife.

How do you do that? It's all about the little things, guys. Call home when you're at the store and ask your wife, "Is there anything you need?" Take your wife out, but make sure *you* call and get the baby-sitter. Don't make her do all the planning for your nights out. Clean up the kitchen so your wife won't even be tempted to do it. Take care of the laundry. Make the bed. Try to think of all the little things your wife does that you have previously taken for granted.

As a new mom, your wife has become a member of what I call "The Order of the Velcro Women": Every need ultimately sticks to her. Dinner and a movie will sound great, but even better if *you* set it up. She might need you to clear your schedule on Thursday nights so she can go work out or have some space and time for herself. If you're starting to frown, stop there. I know you're already seeing less of your wife, and now I'm telling you to let her out even more! But trust me on this one: It'll come back to you. In her heart she'll say, *I'm so glad I married that man,* and she'll love you even more intensely for it. And guys, our wives often have very creative and fun ways of letting us know how much they appreciate us!

Act as her protector.

Everybody will want to come and see the baby, everybody will call your wife on the phone, and she may feel obligated to accommodate all of these visits and requests. (This is especially true since women, in general, tend to be "pleasers" by nature. They don't want to hurt anyone's feelings and think deeply about long-term consequences of even small slights in relationships.) But as her protector, you need to be the one who looks out for her interests. Intercept the phone calls and make yourself the bad guy: "I'm sorry. She is really tired and can't come to the phone right now. But I'll tell her you called. I'm sure she'll call you back as soon as she has a moment."

35

You don't have to be a rocket scientist to know which friends your wife will want to talk to and which ones will be a "chore." Screen the calls accordingly. Likewise, you know which visitors will truly encourage and lift your wife's spirits and which ones will create more work. Who wants to have someone over if you have to work to make yourself and your home presentable for "company," to have a colorful snack or a gourmet meal ready, or to sit and be hospitable when all you're longing to do is sleep? In contrast, a friend who offers to watch the baby or to do your wash and ironing while your wife naps would probably be most welcome. So become the firewall to protect your wife's best interests. Some friends may call you "controlling" and say even worse things behind your back, but deep in her heart, your wife really wants you to be her protector. Because of the way God made her—to be concerned first about everyone else, before herself—she *needs* you. When she sees you looking after her welfare, she'll rest easier, thinking, *He knows me; he can protect me. We'll get through these first crazy days—together.*

Think of how you can help—practically.

No, you can't help with breast-feeding. You're just not wired to do that! But besides traditional household chores, try to think of things you wouldn't normally think of doing, such as writing the thank-you letters for baby-shower gifts. Anticipate needing extra time to focus on caring for your wife, and leave your work at the office. This isn't the time to have a "night out" with the boys.

If you're reading this in anticipation of the birth or receiving a "chosen child," finish up that handyman list a couple weeks before the due date so you'll be free to help out more at home. You need to make room in your schedule. Your golf handicap might go up a bit, and your lawn might grow a little longer, and yeah, a few weeds may crop up in your garden—but none of that matters as much as supporting your wife in these early, crucial days. When our firstborn's due date came near, I knew my life was going to change, but I didn't realize how much it would change. Having that baby in our home changed our family dynamics forever. I was so excited the last month I didn't do much; in retrospect, I wish I had done more to get ready.

Realize how crucial your role as father is.

I hope you realize the influence you can be on this new child. If you have a daughter, you represent all of manhood to your little daughter; you also represent almighty God. Will you be loving, will you be there for her, will you take the time to make an indelible imprint on this young girl's soul? I hope you'll consider picking up a copy of my book *What a Difference a Daddy Makes*. I've found that the type of man a woman chooses to marry is often directly related to the type of relationship she had with her father. The fact is, you *will* make an imprint on your daughter. The only question is whether it'll be a positive or negative one.

37

"But I'm having a son," some of you are saying. Guess what? You represent to that son what men are all about. As he grows up, he'll watch how you treat your wife; that's probably how he'll treat his wife too. Those choice words you use in a moment of anger? Don't be surprised if a few of those slip out of his mouth too. He will watch you with an almost unnerving intensity, and he'll copy just about everything he sees and hears.

It's an awesome responsibility to step up on that mound and take over, but I bet you're up to it. After all, you're a smart guy. And the fact that you've actually read this far shows me you can go the distance. You can close this game and get the job done. Your wife and child are counting on you. You can do it!

YOUR MOST FAMILIAR FRIEND

Moms, now back to you. Hopefully, the next twenty days will get easier because your husband took the time to read the pages we just devoted to him. If he applies what he reads, I hope you'll make the effort to show him how much you appreciate his help, too. If you're a single mother, don't underestimate the value of getting men you trust—a grandfather, mentor, good friend—involved as early as possible in the life of your son or daughter. Let's be honest: Such men can never replace the importance of a father in your child's life, but they can exhibit qualities—strength, trust, love, friendship—that can impact your son or daughter for a lifetime.

Every mother's most familiar friend these first two weeks is going to be exhaustion. The first words out of Sande's mouth following the birth of our firstborn were "I'm exhausted." She had no idea how tiring giving birth was, and she certainly didn't realize it would be even more tiring when you actually bring the little angel home!

Laura, a single mom who was passionate about choosing a child from overseas, had no idea how exhausting the almost-two-year process would be. After reams of doctor visits, fingerprint checks, next-day packages, multiple copies of paperwork for her dossier, she finally received her referral picture—the sweet face of her baby girl. After almost thirty-six hours of flying and sixteen days on the road, she returned home, exhausted. Her parental journey had just begun, and within three months, she had to return back to work.

Now, how is exhaustion a friend?

Exhaustion teaches you to lean on others.

You can't do everything yourself; you're going to need help. And that means your parents, your husband, your friends, your church family. If people aren't offering, learn how to ask. I've heard of some women (talk about planning!) who cook several weeks' worth of meals before delivery and then freeze the meals so they can take them out once the baby arrives. But many women who are eight or nine months pregnant often don't want to go near a stove or oven. The smell of cooking food and the heat trigger a gag reflex.

In short, you need to develop a support system. The smart mother will talk to other moms in the trenches before she has her baby and figure out for herself what will be best for her in terms of support. Maybe you're lucky enough to have a parent or in-law eager to help. Laura, the single mom, did, and she says four years later that she never could have made it without a loving mother who lived only ten minutes away. But the question is, when will Grandma and Grandpa be most beneficial? Right after the birth or the arrival of the child at home, or two weeks later? They may want to come right away, but you may want time with just you and the child, or you, your husband, and the baby first. So I'm giving you permission to put yourself first in this situation, without feeling guilty. Ask yourself, *What will make me most comfortable?*

How do you find all this out? Talk to your girlfriends who have had babies; talk to your pediatrician. Discuss it with your husband. He may know you better than you realize.

Some women are full-fledged members of the "Selfless Martyrs" club—those who are always eager and willing to help others but refuse to be helped by others. However, when you tackle the task of parenting, you need to let your

39

membership expire. Look at such martyr philosophy from another perspective: It's selfish to rob others of the gift of serving you. Sure, it might be a bit humiliating to ask for help, especially if you're used to doing things for yourself. But some parents, friends, and in-laws will be touched beyond words that you're reaching out to them and are willing to admit that you need their help.

If your baby hasn't been born yet, you really may not be able to imagine just how tired you'll be. The thought of having others bring you meals for two weeks may horrify you. But when the time comes, you may well feel the way so many women have felt: relieved that they didn't have to worry about making a meal in the midst of their transition to parenthood. Having that chore taken away has done wonders in the late afternoon—the time when all mothers of young children feel their energy start to wane.

Whatever your support network is going to be, keep in mind that *you* are the one who makes the final decision, and you have the right to change your mind again, without the guilt. Don't be afraid to tell the soon-to-be grandma, "I think I'm going to want you there right away, when we get home, but please give me the freedom to change my mind at the last minute, okay?" This type of advance planning will give you an easy out if you're unexpectedly feeling okay and would just enjoy a little alone time with you, your husband, and the new baby. Never forget: You're the mom now, so you're in charge. This is a major growing-up step for you. Take the responsibility and run with it.

Don't try to fool yourself into believing that you're the kind of woman who just won't need help (in case you're wondering, yes, I can read some of your minds—caught you, didn't I?). I can guarantee you *will* need help—there's no mother on the planet who doesn't—and it'll go a lot easier for you if you can think all this through before you bring baby home.

Exhaustion reminds you to take the long-term view.

You're going to have this child for a long time, and raising this child will be about making choices every day that will shape your child's character. That means you'll have to re-evaluate your priorities, because there will always be more that you can do; there will always be tasks left undone. Housework will always be there, but the time and energy you preserve to pour into your child will really pay off in your relationship now, and in the future.

In the face of these many unfinished chores and tasks, will you still take time to enjoy your husband and your child?

41

I hope you do.

Remember, the first ten days are all about two things: bond and rest. Rest and bond. Anything else is extra.

3

The Big Three:
Eating, Sleeping, and Crying

A lawyer in her early twenties once confidently told me that when she got married and had kids she'd definitely want to keep working. "What would I do all day with a baby? I'd get bored!" she exclaimed.

At the time I just chuckled, saying something like, "You have no idea." The mere thought that she would "run out of things to do" with a baby simply showed her naïveté.

I checked up on her a decade later. She had gotten married, had a baby, quit her job, and had two more children. Now living with her husband and three kids, she can't even believe that she worried about getting "bored." She can't remember the last time she had the leisure to be bored!

This young woman went from talking about environmental regulations and the intricacies of public law to discussing the timing and quantity of her baby's bowel movements and her baby's sleeping patterns.

It happens all the time. No matter how many degrees you have, once you become a parent, the three biggest issues in your life won't be governmental regulations, public relations, or the meaning of life. It'll be how much your baby needs to eat, how to handle crying, and how much sleep she's getting.

I call these "the big three"—because they are the three biggest issues you'll face during a baby's first year.

HE'S A HUNGRY LITTLE SUCKER!

He looks cute and adorable, doesn't he? But boy, he sure can eat! Your new baby may shock you at the quantity and frequency with which he starts to consume first your milk, if you breast-feed, and then food in general.

Breast-feed or bottle-feed?

Keep in mind, your baby is growing almost by the minute. Every day new components of your child's body—her skeletal structure, her sinuses, and more—are being developed and refined. Good food and nutrition are more important now than ever, and nothing is healthier than mother's milk. This is said not to make you feel guilty if you can't breast-feed (and there are a few occasions in which a mother simply isn't able to breast-feed), but merely to state the facts. Numerous studies have shown that the nutritional and relational benefits of breast-feeding are overwhelming, and the American Academy of Pediatrics recommends breast milk for at least the first year of life.

For the first six months or so of a baby's life, you really have only two choices: breast milk or formula. While it takes several weeks of nursing for a mother's milk to completely develop, the most amazing thing about it is that your milk will actually adapt to your child's needs. That's right! In God's miraculous way, the fat content of your breast milk undergoes subtle changes, not only as the baby grows, but also during an individual time of nursing. No scientist can completely mimic this effect.

Breast-feeding has been shown to help with allergies,

infections, and weight control. It is a natural stimulant for your baby's digestive system. As a bonus, if you have a limited income, there is no more economical way to feed your child. Unless your doctor informs you otherwise, there is no need for any kind of supplements during the first six months of your baby's life.

Breast-feeding can seem terribly difficult to the first-time mother. Just about every new mom breaks down into tears, saying, "I thought this was supposed to be easy. Natural. Why won't it work for me?" But hang in there—it will. It may take a few days for your child to learn how to "latch on," and yes, your baby will need to suck for several days before your milk comes in, although he'll get his share of colostrum. Colostrum is the thicker, darker milk produced by your breasts in the first three days or so of nursing. It's low in fat, high in carbohydrates, protein, and antibodies, and contains a higher concentration of immune factors than your mature milk will. La Leche League International describes it as "a natural and 100% safe vaccine" against later diseases and infections. It will probably take a little longer for your sensitive nipples to adapt to the constant tugging of a hungry baby's mouth. So expect early difficulty instead of being surprised by it. And realize that what you're going through is nearly universal—but the benefits are more than worth the early struggle.

45
• • • • •

How often to feed?

How do you determine the quantity of food your baby is getting?

If you're bottle-feeding, you have an accurate reading down to the half-ounce. But if you're breast-feeding, how do you know how much is coming out of those breasts? The rate of your child's growth is the single best determiner of how much nutrition he's receiving. Your pediatrician will be a great help here. If your baby is growing at a reasonable rate, it's safe to assume that he's getting enough milk. But don't let those height/weight charts at the pediatrician's office scare you. Remember that they're just that—charts that represent the average American baby. Every baby is different. If your baby's weight, height, and head circumference are developing normally and following a traditional curve, even if he's smaller or larger than the average baby on the charts, you have nothing to worry about. If you are concerned, share those concerns right away with your pediatrician who can address your specific case.

On average, a newborn infant should feed six to ten times a day, which translates into once every two to four hours. Any less than six times a day, and your child risks becoming dehydrated. Any more than ten times a day, and your nipples are going to start feeling like chewed-up pacifiers! There are differing opinions on whether a child should be allowed to nurse as long as she wants. I fall somewhere in between on this. Your body can take only so much; after the first two weeks, a baby can get 90 percent of your milk in the first five minutes of feeding (per breast). If you're feeling sore, you can use a finger or pacifier to satisfy your child's sucking needs.

There's a slightly more earthy way to make sure baby is getting enough food—keep a close eye on her diapers. There should be four to six wet ones a day, and after about two weeks of age, three dirty ones every day. This is all based on averages, of course. If you're truly concerned, or if your baby seems to be nowhere near these numbers, check with your pediatrician.

Probably the most frequent question I get about feeding in the early days is whether I believe babies should be fed on demand. When you're talking about an infant, yes, I believe you should feed him when he's hungry. You're going to get lots of advice from others about the "right way" to do this, but keep this in mind: Not a one of us is built the same way. Consider how different you are from your siblings. Remember that brother who packed it in at breakfast, eating a dozen pancakes, who then had nothing but a Coke for lunch, but then pigged out once again at dinner? And maybe you had a sister who barely touched breakfast, ate a full meal for lunch, and had a very light dinner.

We're all different, aren't we? Of course we are! So why should we expect all babies to be the same? Even if you have ten babies, you'll likely have ten different eating preferences. God doesn't have one cookie cutter that he uses to stamp us out. Scripture tells us that your baby was "fearfully and wonderfully made."[2] God himself created this child and watched carefully over him in the womb. Your child is a unique creation; there's no one else like him in all the earth!

This also means that you can't really know ahead of time what kind of an eating schedule your child is going to be on. The best way to establish a "schedule" is to start feeding him whenever he's hungry. You'll quickly notice that his nature will dictate what times of the day he wants to eat.

For some of you, this open-ended schedule may be pretty hard to swallow. You like things to be done by the book; unfortunately, there *is* no book when it comes to a child's personal preferences. Let me put it this way: There is going to be a schedule, but it's TBA—"to be announced." The "announcer" is going to be your son or daughter. Believe me, babies have a way of making their desires known! Once you understand his natural rhythm, you and baby can get used to a certain schedule.

The comforting news is that as you become familiar with

your child's schedule, the eating wars will stop. Just about every baby wants to be fed soon after waking up, but when he's hungry again after that depends largely on the child. Read your baby like a book, and then stick to that schedule. You'll find out soon enough that parenting is a balance between legitimately staying in control and also being sensitive to your child's needs.

If you have further questions, consult your pediatrician. Just be wary of any rigid system that says, "This is the way it has to be done" or that tries to construct some "divine method" that every baby must follow. Speaking as a psychologist, I want to assure you that you are not going to mess up your kid based on her feeding schedule. How and when you feed her won't create a spoiled child, a cranky child, or a strong-willed child. These are all valid concerns, but they have nothing to do with early infant feeding.

How can you get a burp?

Part of feeding your child is getting good at producing a mother's favorite sound: a baby's burp. Every infant needs to be burped after every feeding, but if you can't produce a burp, don't force it. Right now you're not a real expert in burping, but you're about to become one. You'll be amazed at how good you'll eventually be at bringing forth that cute little "bubble." Early on you'll probably be a little too soft with your pats, but that's okay. I'd rather you be too gentle than too forceful with a young infant. In time you'll learn what your baby needs to get that bubble out. Trial and error is your best guide here because every baby is different.

Breast-fed babies should be burped before nursing from the other breast. Bottle-fed babies need to make a good bubble after taking in one to two ounces of formula. The three most common burping positions are the following:

1. Baby's head is draped over your shoulder, your left hand holding baby's bottom while your right hand gently pats baby's back.

2. Baby lies across your thighs, face to the side, while you gently pat her back.

3. Baby sits on your lap while you support her with one hand and gently pat her back with the other hand.

Enjoy the bonding!

After you feed your baby, please don't rush off to clean up. If you're at home and you're breast-feeding, don't feel the need to button up your shirt. Take a few minutes and complete the bonding process. Cuddle your child close, notice how she smells, and look at those big, beautiful baby eyes. Touching your baby is such a wonderful gift; next to food and air, touching is probably the third most important element in your child's life right now.

This is a time where you begin this lifelong journey of tactile stimulation. All of us like to be touched. But as we get older, we make it more difficult for others to touch us. So enjoy this time when baby makes it so very easy and convenient to stay connected. Pray for your little boy or girl; sing your favorite songs; giggle and laugh and rub her tummy. Babies love to hear their parents laugh!

SLEEPY TIME

Whew! We just spent all that time talking about eating, and now we're jumping right into sleeping. Are you exhausted yet? Well, don't worry. You may be new at being a mommy, but your baby is also new at being a baby. Together you can get through this.

Help baby adjust to nighttime.

As a psychologist, I love it when parents bring the new baby into their bedroom and have him sleep in a little bassinet right by the bed. Sleeping in the same room for the first few weeks provides a wonderful bonding time, spares you the hassle of having to walk across the house to retrieve your crying infant, and has the added benefit of making any husbandly attempts to act as if he's really sleeping through that cry less than believable.

Check with your pediatrician to determine on what side you should lay your baby in the bassinet since the recommendations tend to shift, and even professionals can disagree. In fact, most are now saying there is no "perfect position" for a sleeping baby, so it's best to leave a decision like this with those who are most up-to-date on changing research.

As an aside, if you have a pediatrician, don't be shy about taking a good chunk of time to talk things through. He or she will expect to spend a longer period of time with a first-time mother. At your first office meeting, there is no reason you should feel compelled to leave without having all your questions answered. A good pediatrician will affirm your interest and patiently answer all the questions you have.

Many moms ask me why their baby cries at night instead of sleeping. It may surprise you that contemporary research suggests that babies don't become particularly light sensitive until about five or six months, which explains why your child can sleep soundly in the noon light and seem raring to go at midnight. Nighttime doesn't mean much to a baby, not like it does to an adult.

Secondly, think of this from the baby's perspective: She's just come out of a soft, warm body—yours or her birthmom's—and everything is new. She gets cuddled all day, listens to Mommy talk, feels secure because your comforting body is always nearby. Then suddenly, at the end of the day, she's shut off in a strange and dark room all by herself.

How would you like that? Particularly if you were too young to fully understand the difference between night and day? *You* know you're coming back to her in the morning, but how does *she* know that? (In the first few months of life, babies don't understand object permanence; when something is removed from their sight, they think it has disappeared.) She's just a baby; she's been with you all day, and suddenly she's alone, with little experience to know that you'll come back. Thinking about it this way kind of puts the crying in a brand-new light, doesn't it?

51
· · · · ·

Once you begin to get your baby on a bit of a schedule—say two to three weeks after birth—you can think about moving her into her own room. Fourteen days is enough time for the baby to make her psychological adjustment to being in this world, and you need to preserve a bit of space that's all your own. If you're worried that moving your baby will hinder you from hearing her crying cues, purchase a baby monitor.

Realize that babies sleep in chunks.

Here's the bad news: Nobody can *make* a child go to sleep. But there's also good news: Sleep is a very natural process, and the average baby will sleep from fifteen to seventeen hours a day. The problem is, these hours will be broken up into very uneven chunks. Many babies will sleep during the day and be fussy at night. Over time—and we're talking weeks, not days here—you can gradually help your child shift the greater proportion of her sleeping hours to nighttime. But for the first two months, five hours of uninterrupted sleep will seem like heaven. Go ahead and wake baby up if her late-afternoon nap is running too long, but don't cut out the late-afternoon nap altogether. Your child's tummy will need food every three to four hours, so there's little chance of you getting a complete night's sleep anyway.

First-time parents have a tendency to make these natural sleep rhythms more difficult than they need to be. I've talked to many moms who have developed elaborate rituals to lull their child to sleep; they may start an hour-long ritual, such as rocking babies in a rocking chair. But I caution you not to start a habit that you don't want to continue forever. Once your child gets used to a routine, it's important to maintain it, so the simpler, the better.

Getting the child to sleep is only half the battle, of course. Many times a greater concern is keeping your child asleep through the night. One time I was speaking at a conference and someone asked me, "Dr. Leman, did you sleep well?"

"Like a baby," I answered. "I woke every two hours."

Every baby is different, of course, but as a rule, they sleep a lot and they wake up a lot. The challenge is that for many babies, the sleep schedule they choose won't be ideal for either Mom or Dad. Your baby doesn't really understand the meaning of Dad or Mom needing to get six or seven hours of sleep before they go to work, and it's the rare baby who sleeps six or seven hours at a stretch shortly after coming home from the hospital. In fact, your pediatrician will proba- bly tell you to wake your baby up for at least one night feed- ing during the first two weeks that you're home.

That's one of the many reasons, I'm convinced, God's design for the family is to have both a mommy and a daddy. I'm not saying you can't make it as a single parent, but it's definitely tougher. If you have a husband, you can tag team, even if husbands do have the innate ability, as we talked about earlier in this book, to play possum in the middle of the night. Though we men have, over the centuries, carefully developed and honed the skill of not flinching even one muscle when our wives glance to see if we're awake, I would like to remind you of a Leman axiom I tell men all over the country: It's only fair that if we daddies were there for the launching, we're there for the landing as well. And that goes for those who help to conceive children biologically as well as those who conceive children through choosing them in the process of adoption. A husband is very capable of giving great paternal love to his son or daughter, which has the added benefit of giving a wife a chance to catch up on the sleep she so desperately needs.

53
• • • • •

Some husbands may try the ruse, "I have to work tomorrow while you get to stay home and sleep," but they say this only because they've never stayed home all day and so probably don't realize how little sleep you get. I realize it's a difficult time of life. Both of you are going to be tired and neither of you will get as much sleep as you think you need. But what you're going through and what you're asking your husband to go through is a normal passage of life that women and men have been going through for centuries. It won't last forever.

That doesn't mean it won't occasionally *feel* like forever, of course! When the baby is sick and has a cold, you probably won't sleep well because the baby isn't sleeping. There's something about moms that seems to connect their ability to sleep with their infant's. You might have the steamer going to help baby breathe, but I bet you're still waking up at every cough.

Sande and I have certainly been there. Little Hannah was a dream child but had colic for about six months. Colic will severely test the patience of the most devout saint who has ever walked on this fair earth. Your baby doesn't sleep well so she's constantly fussy; you're not sleeping well, so you're constantly irritable; your spouse isn't sleeping well, so the two of you tend to bicker with each other. . . . It goes on and on. You may find yourself asking, "Why did I ever decide to do this? What were we thinking? It's nothing but hard work."

These are normal feelings, and they do pass with time. Fortunately, colic is sort of like adolescence: It doesn't last forever (it just feels like it).

54   **Find—and adjust to—your baby's natural rhythm.**

Day sleeping is similar to eating—every child is different. Develop a schedule based on what you see in your baby, and once that schedule naturally forms, try to stay to it. You have to bend your schedule around your child's if you want consistency. In other words, if your baby usually goes to sleep at 7:30 P.M., don't take her to a class that starts at 7:00 P.M. or leave for the mall after 6:00 P.M. Plan your day around baby's sleep schedule, and both of you will be much happier because you'll soon fall into a predictable rhythm.

A lot of mothers get upset that their babies can be so fussy at certain times of the day. I say, "Get used to it and deal with it!" Most of this frustration stems from the fact that Mom has not taken the time to get to know her baby's natural rhythm, and she has tried to make her baby work around her own schedule. Just because you can wake up at 6:00 A.M. to get ready and go to work doesn't mean your baby can adapt to your schedule. It might not be convenient for you to put baby to bed at 7:00 P.M. and wake up with her at 4:00 A.M., but you're only asking for trouble if you plan a big gathering that doesn't get started until after 7:00 P.M., and then get frustrated that your baby is so fussy. Of course she's fussy—she's tired, and it's past her bedtime!

The good news is that sleep schedules change quickly. The first ten days will be a lot different than the first ten months, and the routines won't really stop changing until your child is done with her naptimes. By two months, your child will be physically capable of sleeping through the night without being fed. By three or four months, most babies (but by no means all) should sleep either through one nighttime feeding or through the entire night. At that point, you can be a little bolder about letting him cry. It's your job to help distinguish between naptime and bedtime so that junior can begin to get a feel for what's going on. To do this, create a new ritual for bedtime—give baby a bath, sing a special song, darken the room, give baby a special toy or blanket. Do something that signifies this is different from a typical nap— and stick with it, but remember to keep it manageable, timewise.

55

Just remember: You're the mother. You are in charge. If baby starts to sleep more during the day than the night, it's your job to get him turned around. Get him up from his afternoon nap, play with him a little more vigorously before you put him down so he's extra tired and ready for nighttime, and feed him a little extra. You may have to help your child find an acceptable sleep rhythm.

CRYING

Memo to moms: Babies cry. That's what they do.

Crying is part of human experience. I cry reading the sports pages or when looking at what's happening to my 401(k) when the stock market free-falls. Sometimes I cry when my accountant tells me what I owe the IRS. I bet you've even cried over a few really sappy commercials.

Over time, you've learned when it's appropriate and even healthy to cry, and when you need to be more guarded. You've also learned how to cry without expecting the world to stop or yelling as if your house were on fire.

Baby hasn't learned all that yet. She will cry for many different reasons. Maybe she's wet, maybe she's uncomfortable, maybe a piece of clothing is pinching her body, maybe she doesn't like the position she's in, maybe she's hungry or tired, or maybe she just needs to shed a little excess energy.

56

Learn to "read" your child's cries.

The important thing is that you know your baby so well that you learn to "read" her cries. It's like this: In the summertime we live in New York state, and we share our summer home with dozens of ducks. I'd hate to tell you what I spend on crack corn; our ducks love that stuff, so I buy it in 50- and 75-pound bags. That keeps the ducks coming around. And as I watch them, it's amazing to me how well mother ducks know their ducklings. Usually the ducks come up to our house in families. Though I like ducks, I have to admit that if you've seen one duck, you've seen them all. They're hard to tell apart—but mama ducks know their little ones!

If a mallard should approach one of those little ducklings, the normally mild-mannered momma duck turns into a pit bull. She'll lower her shoulder like an NFL linebacker and charge, pulling tail feathers out of the mallard's behind, squawking as she goes! Some of these moms have from eight to a dozen ducklings. The mom is always upright, looking around, keeping track of each of her children, though they are mixed into other groups.

That's what you need to be like—so attuned to your child that you can pick her cry out of a nursery or group of children. I've met many moms who, over a period of time, are able to detect the slight difference in a hungry cry from, say, a dirty-diaper cry. The difference might seem undetectable to other people, including the husband, but as a mother you'll pick up on that and be right nine times out of ten. You'll be able to tell when your baby is letting loose with an "attention-getting cry" and when she really is in pain or discomfort.

Realize babies need to cry.

Let me assure you that just like establishing an eating schedule, you needn't worry about damaging your child's psyche by letting him cry. The fact is, babies *need* to cry. It's healthy for them physically, and until they can speak, it's the easiest way to communicate. When dealing with a very young infant, I think it's best to respond immediately to crying. As the child gets into the first two months of life, though, you need to pull back a little bit.

I say this because in dealing with your baby's cries, you need to find balance. On the one hand, your baby is a hedonistic little sucker who will wrap you around her tiny little finger if you let her. On the other hand, she is completely dependent on you and has a difficult time—especially since you're a first-time parent—letting you know exactly what it is that she needs.

If you comfort your baby every time she grimaces or frowns, you're probably going overboard. If you're hovering over your child, responding to everything she does, you're going to train her that being fussy is the best way to get attention.

Just relax. Sometimes when babies are laid down to sleep, they'll cry, and that's okay. Let them cry. Most healthy babies will cut down their crying within a couple of days if crying doesn't elicit the hoped-for response.

If you're dealing with an older baby—say four or five months old—and she is crying, check her diaper, consider when she's had her last meal, think about whether she could be tired, feel for a temperature, and make sure no piece of clothing is pinching her. If everything appears to be okay, assume that your baby just needs to cry—and let her. Some babies need to cry before they can fall asleep.

Recently an experienced mother of four gave me a pearl of insight: "I just needed to learn that sometimes babies cry for no good reason, and there's nothing I can do about it. I used to take it personally whenever my baby was the slightest bit unhappy, as if I could 'cure' everything. But you know what? My husband loves me, but he can't take away my headache, stomachache, or cramps! I can put ointment on my baby's bottom when she gets diaper rash, but there's still going to be some discomfort. It's unrealistic to think that you can have a baby who is perpetually happy. As long as we live in the real world, there are going to be disappointments, limitations, and occasional hurts and pains. Both babies and mothers have to learn how to live with them."

You're not a failure as a mom if your baby cries a lot. Don't take it personally. Every baby cries at least an hour a day, and some can cry for up to four hours a day. *Above all, never shake your baby to get her to stop crying, and never spank an infant.* This won't tell baby that you're "really serious," it will only agitate her all the more—and risk serious brain damage at the same time. If you find yourself losing control because constant crying is driving you crazy, call your husband, a friend, or a neighbor immediately and be honest: "I really need a break or I'm afraid I may hurt this child.

Could you come over?" There isn't a mother on the planet who doesn't get frustrated sometimes, so you're not a bad mom. But since you're the adult, it's important for you to be proactive, asking for relief from exhaustion and crying jags, rather than reactive, taking out your frustration on the baby, who is simply doing "what's natural." We'll talk more about this in chapter 4, "The First Year."

Try these techniques.

Remember that every child will respond differently, but here are some proven techniques to deal with crying. If one doesn't work, try the next one!

- Rock baby in a rocking chair.
- Wrap baby tightly in a blanket.
- Hold baby and sway gently side-to-side.
- Sing songs to baby or play soft music.
- Give baby a warm bath.
- Take baby for a car or stroller ride.
- Lay baby down with a hot-water bottle that's soothingly warm to the touch.
- Give baby a relaxing massage, using baby lotion.
- Use a pacifier. Today's versions are very teeth-friendly.
- Try a baby swing, particularly one that has a ticktock sound.

If you start to get too tired, here's a helpful exercise: Go to the calendar, take a pen in hand, count out eight weeks from today, and make a big circle. Sometime around that circle, your baby will finally sleep through the entire night. As long as she's fed and burped right before she goes to bed, she'll be able to make it to the morning, giving you your first night's rest in a long time. Your baby's night may only be six or seven hours long, but it'll be more than the two or three hours of an infant.

Occasionally, I've met moms who haven't had a full night of sleep in over a year, especially since the last few months of pregnancy aren't particularly restful. Just keep reminding yourself that this, too, will pass. You might feel like a full-time waiter, maître d', and farmhand all rolled up into one, but it's going to get better. I guarantee it.

PRECIOUS TIME

How well your child is navigating the big three—eating, sleeping, and crying—will greatly influence your level of satisfaction the first six months of your child's life. If she is eating well, getting at least five to six hours of sleep at night, and crying only when necessary, you're going to feel like one of the luckiest women on the face of the earth.

Others of you are going to have a baby who gorges on breast milk, immediately spits it up, and then demands to eat again, even though you're convinced the gas tank is empty. Unfortunately, your baby isn't convinced and is determined to turn your breasts into pacifiers. These same babies tend to wake you up repeatedly throughout the night.

Here's the true challenge: As a first-time parent, you don't really know if your baby is easy or difficult, because you don't have anyone to compare this child to. Some of you will be surprised how easy baby number one is compared to baby number two, if you have other children down the road. Some of you will realize that behavior you thought was extraordinary is actually pretty normal, and you'll lower your expectations for your other children. But comparing your friend's or your sister's baby, who doesn't live with you, to yours is like comparing watermelon with grapes—babies act differently at different times of the day. You live with your baby twenty-four hours a day, seven days a week.

Regardless of whether your baby seems difficult or easy, I hope you hold on to this season as a very precious time. This is your first time as a parent, and you will never have another time like it. It will be different with a second child and almost a matter of routine with your third and (if you choose to keep going) your fourth or fifth child. But you'll never have another time quite like this one.

In spite of how tired you are now, one day you'll look back on this time with great fondness; it may even bring tears to your eyes. The exhaustion won't feel so intense; the frustration will be a bit removed; and you'll probably laugh about how you took everything so seriously and carried antibacterial soap with you everywhere you went. But you'll miss these days. You may not want to relive them, but you'll miss them.

Trust me, you will.

4

The First Year

Welcome to the Ferris wheel of postbirth emotions!

This is as good a time as any to broach an important topic for those of you who have recently birthed your firstborn: If you charted your hormones and emotions right now, they'd look like the stock market—up one minute, climbing a peak the size of Mount Everest, only to take a dive into Death Valley the next. So what's happening?

Following a birth, your hormones are all over the map. Estrogen levels are dropping drastically; progesterone is falling too, as is thyroid function. To make matters worse, certain mood-controlling hormones—like dopamine and serotonin—drop as well. In short, all the extra chemical lift that your body released to help you get through pregnancy and childbirth is now being flushed out of your system. The giant, sucking feeling you're experiencing is not in your head—it's a physiological fact. One moment you can't keep yourself from kissing your baby. Two hours later you feel emotionally dead and are sitting there in the dark while baby cries away; you feel unable to muster up the energy to check on her.

THE BABY BLUES

Do you feel exhausted? insecure? angry—but you don't know why? paranoid and fearful? sad?

These are normal emotional mood swings that some new mothers pass through. Though they can be quite distressing, they are nothing to get overly concerned about. Postpartum blues (sometimes called "baby blues") occurs in about 80 percent of new mothers, resulting in significant mood swings during the first few weeks you bring baby home. So relax—you're not alone in these feelings. If you've chosen your child through adoption, you may experience similar emotions (though not from a change in hormones) from the stress of life change, lack of sleep, and general exhaustion due to the responsibility for this new member of your family.

What you've heard about in the news, through stories of women who have harmed their own children is entirely different—and a more serious matter. It's called postpartum depression and is more rare than you might think—occurring only in about two out of every thousand new mothers. Such depression, like other cases of diagnosed depression, requires therapeutic care. For instance, I've had a couple of patients who had psychotic reactions to birth. One mother rushed her baby to the hospital, convinced that her child was dead. Doctors looked the baby over and declared that the infant was just fine. On her third such trip, the doctors finally clued in to what was going on and prescribed the right drugs and counseling—for the *mother*.

During the first year it's a really good idea to talk to a friend who's been through the experience of mothering a young child. Or join a new mother's group (MOPS—Mothers of Preschoolers—is only one such group), where you will get lots of perspectives—and find comfort for the shared areas of struggle that moms face.

Don't expect your husband to understand. No offense—but he's a guy. He's never gone through the physical experience of birthing a baby and having his body chemical makeup altered. And as a parent to either a birthed or chosen child, he as a man will never go through quite the emotional seesaw that you experience with your child on a daily basis. Besides, if you're in the baby-blues stage, most likely your husband is taking the brunt of your sudden anger and down-swings and may need his own outlet—to talk with other fathers who've been through the ropes! So you *need* to talk to another mom who can understand what you're going through.

So if suddenly your baby is driving you up the wall or you're treating your husband as your number-one enemy, suspect baby blues as the culprit. The ones closest to you are the most likely to bear the brunt of your mood swings. If you start to feel suicidal or you have thoughts of harming your baby, seek therapeutic help immediately. Don't make major or rash decisions during this period. Realize that some of the hostility you feel may be based on stress and hormones— more than an accurate reflection of your feelings.

65

I can't give you a surefire prescription to climb out of these downtimes, because every woman has a different remedy. Some of you would do well to start working out again, or just go on a long walk through the woods. Exercise may be your best medicine. Others of you need to laugh—rent some funny movies or, even better, go out to the cinema. Maybe you need a hot bath with a good novel. Though I know weight may be a concern at this point, consider giving your-self a treat of some sort: chocolate, ice cream, or other "comfort" food. Don't overdo it, but give yourself the free-dom to pamper yourself a bit. Getting out in the sun is quite often a great tonic; there's something about sunshine that seems to reach our souls.

Just as your body is physically recovering, so your mind needs to adjust to the major change that has just taken place.

You've gone from being a baby, to being an adolescent, to being an adult, to being a mother with a key responsibility for another life. Give yourself room to adjust. You've just passed through one of the most significant passages of life. And you're juggling more things now than you thought possible before this child became yours. In this chapter we'll talk about a few of the key areas—like menus and schedules, talking and reading time, discipline, and playtime.

YOUR BABY'S MENU AND SCHEDULE

About midway through your child's first year, you can begin introducing your baby to solid foods. I recommend you consult with your pediatrician on the best time to do this for your particular baby. Because of a baby's tongue-thrust reflex, an infant younger than four months will usually not be able to take solid food; she'll just push it out of her mouth with her tongue. But by five months, that reflex should be gone.

Once again, I'm speaking as a psychologist rather than a medical doctor, so from that perspective I want to stress that you should not let early feedings degenerate into power struggles. If your six-month-old doesn't seem to want solid food, there's no point in embarrassing yourself with all kinds of airplane antics to sneak the food into his mouth. Go back to breast-feeding or formula, and try again a day or two later.

Also, don't expect too much too soon. In other words, don't set yourself up for failure. Your baby has never eaten solid foods before. If you can take her in your lap, and she takes half a spoonful on the first try, then spits out the second, you've made progress. Stop there and try again later.

You've heard it before in this book, but I'll say it again: First-time parents have a tendency to be overly nervous and to try to make baby fit a certain regimented schedule. But remember this: As long as your baby is getting proper nutrition and growing at an acceptable level, it's not a "Life-and-death" issue whether they start taking solids at six months or seven months.

If you want meals to be enjoyable, why start an early habit of feeding wars?

I've been very pleased with the way my wife helped our kids in this area. Sande used the food processor to make her own baby foods, mashing up vegetables and other menu items to create in our children a taste for a variety of types of food. As teenagers, our kids actually fought over the broccoli. Now, you may not have the time, opportunity, or inclination to mash up food for your baby for every meal. But the point is this: Your kids will discover sugar soon enough. Coca-Cola, Pepsi, and the Mars candy company will spend billions of advertising dollars to make sure of that. There's certainly no need to rush it. By cutting down on the sugar and feeding your child healthy foods, it's less likely that you'll face the food wars that so many parents want to discuss with me in the counseling room. Kids get hungry, and they'll eat what's there if nothing else is available to them. The sooner they acquire a taste for healthy food, the less chance there will be for the toddler food wars that might erupt a year or two later.

67

If you've adopted an older baby or toddler, especially one from a different country, the child may already have some acquired likes and dislikes, or at least things that are familiar or not familiar. The best plan for broadening your child's horizon menu-wise may be to feed him the foods you know he likes, and then gradually, one at a time, introduce some bites of "new to his tastebuds" food in a fun, relaxed setting. Force-feeding your child will only spark the food wars you're trying to avoid.

WHEN SHOULD BABY TALK?

As the mother, you will greatly influence your child's ability to communicate. Your baby will hear you speak more than anyone else, and she'll learn to follow your speech patterns. The best way to teach baby to talk is to model your own speech carefully. Baby talk is okay early on, but you should completely switch to normal speech by the sixth month.

When dealing with an infant, I think it's best to avoid pronouns (I, you, me) and instead use names or titles:

"Does Samantha want to eat? Is Samantha hungry?"

"Daddy's home! Can you see Daddy?"

"Give Mommy a kiss!"

Doing this will eventually show your child that everyone has a name. Your baby should understand her own name by about the fifth month and the word *no* somewhere near the ninth month. By ten months, your infant should begin responding to spoken requests, showing that she understands what you're saying. And between ten and eighteen months, you can look forward to hearing baby's first words. (Babies begin babbling much earlier than this, and many first-time parents may "interpret" these babbles as actual words—but in most cases, a four- or five-month-old "saying" a word just got lucky putting the right sounds together.)

Since you're a first-time parent, I can't stress this enough: Every baby develops at his own pace, and the pace of development does not directly correlate to I.Q. Just because your baby doesn't start talking until eighteen months doesn't mean she is less intelligent than the neighbor baby who started speaking words at ten months. Some babies develop gross motor skills before language or vice versa. There need be no "race" between babies.

However, if your child hasn't started speaking any words by eighteen months, you might want to have a professional check everything out. Before the age of eighteen months, just relax and keep playing games and enjoying your baby. Your pediatrician can listen to your baby's sounds much earlier than that and assure you that she is on a normal developmental pattern.

Here's the irony: Many parents who have worried, "When will my child talk?" have a few months later said, "When will she shut up?" Kind of puts talking in perspective, doesn't it?

READ, READ, AND READ MORE!

One of the most wonderful things a parent can do for a baby is read to him. So get a chunky baby book, put baby on your lap, and read aloud. This activity builds intimacy and bonding between the two of you, involves tactile stimulation, and helps develop baby's understanding of speech.

Babies love to look at books—especially ones that have pictures of other babies. They like picture books, and their favorite subject is usually other babies. And today, thankfully, publishers publish cloth books that are ideal for infants because they can be washed and are soft to the touch. With a young infant, you're not trying to teach them to read. You're getting them used to the sounds that words make. As they get older, you can use these same books for elementary teaching: "Where's your nose? your mouth? your lips?"

DISCIPLINE

We'll talk a lot more about this topic later on when we discuss toddlers, but there are a few things I want to mention here, as there is a difference between disciplining an infant and disciplining a toddler.

The best overall discipline with young kids who are still beginning to talk and just starting to walk is to simply pick them up and remove them from what they're doing. Kids are naturally curious; don't read too much into their actions. Simply distract them and avoid the power play.

Work hard at minimizing the word *no*. First-time parents in particular use the word *no* so often that babies are anesthetized to it by the time they're six months old. I know a dog trainer who told me that he rarely uses the word *come* when training a dog, because the word was ruined before the trainer ever got to the dog. A good trainer will never repeat a command, but by the time a dog is three months old, he's already heard, "Come here, Rosie, come here. Come on, come here. That's it. Come here!" The word *come* means nothing to the dog at that point. If she disobeyed it without consequence for the first few months of her life, it will be extremely difficult to train her using that same word. It's far more effective to choose a different word altogether.

The same principle holds true for parents, babies, and the word *no*. It's overused. In fact, get another word for the big issues, because you're going to need it when there's greater urgency. If baby has picked up a nice pillow, for example, and you say, "No, no, put the pillow down," there isn't a compelling reason for the one-year-old baby to consider the word *no* any more important as he pokes a fork into the electrical outlet! You want a word that is reserved for true urgency, said with such a force that it will at least make your baby jump.

Parents often talk about "baby-proofing" their home, referring to making it safer. But I think it's just as important to baby-proof your home so as to avoid unnecessary discipline. Remove the fragile items that will draw a young child's natural attention. When they do grab something they shouldn't have, slip to diversion: Give them something else, and they'll usually forget about the forbidden item right away. Engage your child with boundaries and limits while working hard to create an environment that isn't unnecessarily tempting. If I'm on a diet, I don't want ice cream in the house. If I've got a young child, I'm not going to leave expensive glassware within his reach. Why court temptation?

I don't believe spanking is appropriate under the age of two, and I think it runs its course by the age of six. I used to say eight, but I've been moving younger for years. As soon as a kid is six, there are so many other things you can do besides spanking. The key is to find out what's important to your child—what kind of discipline will make an impact. Some children hate being isolated from you or their siblings, so being told to sit in another room for five minutes by themselves is discipline that really works. Other times it may take losing a privilege—like a special treat, their favorite television program, or a missed birthday party.

71

If you're going to use spanking in any shape or form, always use an open hand on your kid's bottom. Never use anything that would leave a mark in any way. Not only is it illegal, leaving a mark constitutes abuse. Spanking is meant to correct a behavior, not to mark a body. If you hit hard enough to leave a telltale mark, you've gone overboard. That's why you must be in control of your emotions before you spank. You're way too big and way too strong in relation to a small child to be flailing away in anger. If you're not in control of your emotions, don't spank.

That's why I believe that spanking should be very rare. Save it for the "big issues" and true cases of defiance, not simple immaturity. In many cases all it takes from a parent is a stern look or a stern word to stop unwanted behavior.

Other children, even young children, are able to understand
simple explanations as to why you don't want them to
behave a certain way (such as running out into the street).
Our youngest child is now ten years old. She has been
spanked a grand total of one time in her entire life. If all
you're doing for discipline is spanking, something is wrong
with the relationship.

Another caveat here: If you were physically abused as a
child, I recommend that you avoid spanking altogether. The
baggage you're carrying is too great and too dangerous for
you to play on this field. There are other forms of discipline
(see my book *Making Children Mind without Losing Yours*)
that would be more appropriate for you to use.

Keep in mind, of equal importance to the pain of a spanking
is Mom's stern look, the tone of her voice, and her demeanor
that communicates the seriousness of the moment. Your
child will read all of that well enough without being swatted.
While I don't rule out spanking altogether, I think it should be
used only as a last resort and as one component of your entire
response. Before a spanking, however, make sure you explain
age-appropriately to your child why she is being spanked.
This also allows you a minute to take a breath, to cool down,
and to think straight before you act.

After a spanking, you need to hold your child, put her on
your shoulder, and reassure her that you love her. But also
stress that she can't continue to act that way. Talk calmly
and lovingly, and make the entire episode an event. If you
don't have time to reassure your child and talk about what
happened, don't spank her. To reach out in anger and give
her a quick swat and not follow through with training is, in
my view, very poor parenting. Spanking may be necessary as
part of the process, but it's sheer laziness to use it as the
entire process.

A ONCE IN A LIFETIME OPPORTUNITY

You're entering a very special year. Never again, in all your life, will you spend another first year as a first-time mom with your firstborn. So hold onto it.

Once your infant becomes a few months old, you really see personhood begin to develop. So enjoy this process. Get a feel for the personality God has given your child. Every kid has her own quirks. Our second daughter, Krissy, picked the fuzz off her blankie, made a ball of it, and stuck it in her nose and ear. None of our other kids did that (thank goodness!), but Krissy loved it.

Every kid has her own individual birth print. And this little firstborn likes things in a very particular way. You'll find, for example, that your little one might love your hips. You're worried about them getting big, but big hips make great little cradles and resting places, and babies love to bounce. Each child will find a place on your body that for whatever reason feels good and comfortable. When you have more children, you'll find that child number two and child number three will probably pick a different spot. So adjust accordingly—and just enjoy.

73
• • • • •

During the first ten days, we stressed how important it was for you to rest and bond. Following that time, during this first year I want you to keep enjoying your child. And that means lots of unhurried bonding and playtime. Babies love games—and the simplest games seem to be their favorites. I believe so wholeheartedly in playing with young children that I've included some classic "Favorite Baby Games" at the back of this book (see page 00). Try these, and create some of your own, too. As you play together, it won't take long before you find your baby's play rhythm. You'll discover what uniquely makes her laugh. So laugh it up—

together. It will be time well invested in your lifetime relationship.

This is going to be a very special year in your life and in the life of your baby, so enjoy it!

5

The Ten Most Common
First-Time Parenting Mistakes

In my counseling room, over the radio, and in seminars all over North America, I've spoken to countless first-time parents. Over the decades, I've become as familiar with early parenting mistakes as medical doctors have become familiar with common diseases. Here are the mistakes first-time parents are most likely to make—and what you can do if you see yourself falling into them.

1. A CRITICAL EYE

What's your standard for behavior? Is it perfection? Is your goal to create a computerized mannequin that will do whatever you say, as soon as you say it?

If so, let me ask you a question. When is the last time *you* had a perfect day? When is the last twenty-four-hour stretch where you didn't utter a single cross word or respond a bit slowly to just one request? When have you maintained a positive attitude throughout the *entire* day?

There's a reason I've chosen this as the very first trap a first-time parent is likely to fall into. You've never raised a child before. You're thinking like an adult. Your tendency is going to be to try to raise the "perfect" child, and you may bury your son or daughter under your high expectations.

Never forget that training takes time and that the standard isn't perfection. When you cook a meal, is it always perfect? When you parallel park your car, is it the regulation eighteen inches away from the sidewalk, both tires equally distant from the curb? When you iron a pair of pants, is every pleat perfectly creased?

I doubt it. A lot of times we have to settle for "good enough." So why won't parents do this with their kids?

Here's a common scenario. First-time mom tells Rebecca, "Becky, I want you to go in and make your bed." Four-year-old Becky does what she's told. Mom comes in, sees one little bump, pulls on the bedspread, notices that one side is slightly longer than the other, readjusts the covers, fluffs the pillows, and turns to her now very discouraged child.

"Good job, Becky," Mom says—but her actions gave a very different message. No matter what that mom says to Becky, Becky is going to think, *I messed up again*. Your words may say one thing, but when your actions say something else, guess which one your kid will believe? The one that says "You don't measure up."

Moms do this all the time. In a few years your child is going to learn how to read. He'll get two sentences perfectly but mispronounce one word in the third sentence. Too many first-time moms will immediately jump in and say, 'Oh no, Michael, that's a long *e* sound. Try it again.'"

When child number four makes a similar mistake, you and your husband will laugh. "Isn't that cute? He says 'selletins' instead of 'skeletons.'" The reason you'll laugh is that you'll know your child will eventually get it right. But the firstborn rarely gets this leeway.

As a mom, I hope you choose to be a nurturing, encouraging presence. Outside the home, everybody is going to want a piece of your kid. Teachers want her to help out and get good grades. Playmates want her to join in. Younger siblings want her to help them tie their shoes. If she comes home and Mom makes the same demands—*come on, honey, jump over the high-jump bar of life one more time!*—your kid is going to get very tired by the time she's eighteen.

I particularly want to stress this to you first-time parents because your firstborn child is already going to be highly motivated. When you use conditional love and ask him to jump through hoops before he can eat dinner, you're simply pouring gasoline on an already out-of-control fire.

I know a woman in her late thirties who recently buried her mother. The family had several sisters and one brother, and after the funeral the sisters got together and just talked about their mom. "The house wasn't always clean," they admitted, "and the meals certainly weren't gourmet quality most of the time—but Mom was always there for us. She always took the time to listen, to ask questions, to give us backrubs late at night, and listen to us talk about our problems with school, friends, or boys."

What a wonderful thing to have said about you! This mom put the emphasis where it belonged. She was a nurturing, loving parent, and her kids cherish her memory accordingly. Now, how would you like to hear your kids say this about you: "The house was always spic and span. The meals looked like a spread out of *Gourmet* magazine, but you know what? We could never please that woman, could we? It seemed like she was always more concerned about whether we took our shoes off than how our day went. If we got three A's and two Bs, she wanted to know what happened with the two Bs. At least she can't cluck her throat at us anymore."

Most kids are pushed too hard today. Parents want their

kids to be number one at everything they do. If their kid comes in second in anything, parents are apt to enroll their kid in a special program or give them private tutoring and individual lessons to maintain the illusion that their children really are superior in all things. One of my daughters and her husband are both schoolteachers. Some of the kids who come to their classes are average in intelligence and get average grades—but that's not good enough for Mom and Dad. They create all kinds of waves trying to squeeze something out of their child that just isn't there.

Please, accept your child as he is. He isn't going to excel at everything.

Early on, as soon as your baby can sit up, and then as soon as she can put away toys, you're going to have to choose what your standard will be. Is it perfection?

We could learn a lot from watching a Special Olympics event. All those kids, every one of them running with a smile, seeing everybody get a ribbon at the end—there really is something to that. As kids grow older, they can compete; I want my older kids to learn how to lose. But early on, I don't want to bury them with an unduly high standard of perfection.

Think about this as a part of bonding: Are you drawn to people who have all the answers or to people who are real? Most of us are drawn to people who are real. Your kids are going to be the same way.

One final word on this to those of you who are wives: You're going to have to be watchful of your husband in this regard. Men have a tendency to be too hard and too critical of their firstborn sons. One young man shared with me how his father constantly criticized him as he grew up. The dad either berated his son for being "as stubborn as a mule" or for simply being a rotten kid. The son couldn't remember a single instance of encouragement.

Finally the boy had had enough. After once more being called a mule, he looked the word up in the dictionary.

"Dad," he asked, "do you really think I'm a mule?"

"If you're not a mule," Dad answered, "then I don't know what one is."

"I was just wondering, because I looked up the word *mule* in a dictionary and it said a mule was an animal that had a horse for a mother and a jackass for a father."

Says the son: "He never compared me to a mule again."

2. OVERCOMMITMENT

Maybe I have a jaundiced view of human nature, due to the fact that I'm the guy you call when your family is falling apart. I'm the voice on the radio that you talk to when problems arise. I'm one of the talking heads that ABC's *The View* brings on to discuss troublesome family issues in our day. I'm open to the fact that this may color how I think about things, but even so, I believe statistics bear me out on this.

Your baby is going to grow up into an adolescent. As a fourteen- or fifteen-year-old, she could take drugs and die of an overdose. As a sixteen-year-old, he could have a little too much to drink, get scared about what you'll say, and choose to drive home anyway—and then get in a terrible accident. As a seventeen-year-old high school junior she might have sex and get pregnant; as an eighteen-year-old senior he might get bored and decide to hot-wire some cars, "just for the fun of it," or maybe go out and blow up a mailbox or two—only to be charged with a felony.

What keeps kids from doing things like this? We all know that many kids fall into these traps because we read about them in the newspaper every day. So what are parents doing to keep their kids out of trouble?

79

The most important thing you can do to prevent this needs to be done in your child's earliest years of life. Create a place of belonging and an attitude of family togetherness. When I'm standing in front of a group of people and I say, "Everybody point to yourself," 999 out of 1,000 will point right to their heart. What you have to capture as a parent is your child's heart. You've got to know your child's heart, help train your child's heart, protect your child's heart, and listen to your child's heart. This is more important than making sure your two-year-old is socialized, can play soccer, gets an early start in ballet, and has music-appreciation lessons. Spend the early years enjoying each other's company and use that time to capture your child's heart.

80

Although kids are hedonistic by their nature, they want to be part of a family and they want to identify with their home. Most of us adults have experienced something very similar. You're coming back from a long trip or a long meeting, exhausted and hungry, and one of you says, "Think we should stop and get a bite to eat?" and the other one responds, "I am kind of hungry, but you know what? I just really want to be home. Even if we just eat a bowl of cereal, I want to be home."

And you say, "You know, you're right. Let's go home."

That same yearning lies within our kids. Home is a special place to be. When you choose to live an overcommitted life, you are training your child to identify her heart with what is outside the home. Why do you want to do that?

Another problem with overly busy homes is that the most profound lessons get squeezed out for lack of time. Instead of talking about what's really important, you and your husband spend most of your time talking about who is going to pick up which kid where. Then dinners get squeezed out, and before long, nobody is really talking to anybody anymore. You're too tired, so you turn on the television and continue living separate lives.

Your kids are watching you—do they see you get more excited about catching the latest episode of *The West Wing* or talking about things like your values and your personal faith? Do you let what isn't important over the long-term crowd out what is eternally important? It's *crucial* that parents of faith not only *say* they have faith but practice that faith in ways children can see—every day. It took 9/11 for many in our country to wake up to just how important God is in the life of our nation, and I hope that's a lesson we don't soon forget.

Here's the challenge, however: Just because parents have faith in God is no reason to assume that their kids are going to have that same faith. You need what I call the "great transfer." The best way to achieve this is to consistently and persistently live out your faith in front of your kids. Let them see and hear you praying—and not just at mealtimes. Integrate your faith into your day, as if you're having a "running conversation" with God—rather than waiting to talk to him about "the big things." Show your kids that you don't have to wait until Wednesday night or Sunday to talk to God; he's part of your family every day. But if you're overly busy and try to shortcut the process by force-feeding religion down their throats, you'll likely make them rebel. One family I counseled was surprised when their teenage son refused to go to church. But I couldn't blame the son—he'd been forced to enter the church building every time the church was open, no matter what the event was. By age fifteen, he was sick of the whole "social business" of church, and no wonder.

If you're around your kids enough, however, and they see how you trust in God and include God in your day, and they

81
• • • • •

personally observe how relevant God is in your life, then they can respond to that authentic invitation. As your kids get older, you'll soon find that while they rarely listen to lectures—particularly moral lectures—they also rarely miss life lessons: how Dad speaks when another driver cuts him off on the road; whether Mom encourages or gossips as she talks on the phone.

If you invest time in your family and do things right, your kid, believe it or not, is going to want to please you. If your daughter has a strong family identity, when somebody is passing marijuana around the car, saying, "Try it, you'll like it," she'll say, "I'm a Leman, and we don't do that."

If a group of boys is picking on somebody smaller, and one of your son's friends holds up the hapless fellow and says, "Come on, Jason, it's your turn—hit him in the gut while I hold him," your son will say, "I'm an Alexander, and we don't treat people that way."

You can't give your child a more powerful antidote to negative peer pressure than to create a strong sense of family and values.

"But Dr. Leman, my kid is nine months old! Isn't it a bit early to be talking about all this stuff?"

Not at all—because this strong sense of family and values is created from day one, by keeping your child at home; by not putting her into four or five (or even, at that age, one or two) extracurricular activities; by making the sacrifices necessary to truly bond as a family.

Before your schedule gets out of hand, take a meat cleaver to it; start hacking away. Reserve the best hours and the most important days for your family. Work everything else around that. If nothing else fits, then you have your answer—you have to say no to all other options.

3. NOT ENOUGH VITAMIN *N*

Maybe you've purchased bottles of Fred, Barney, Wilma, and Pebbles Flintstones vitamins to make sure junior gets enough Vitamin B, C, D, and E. Maybe you prefer Sesame Street vitamins, or you choose to go the old-fashioned route and just make sure your kid gets a well-rounded diet.

Good for you.

Just don't forget vitamin N.

"That's a new one, Dr. Leman. I haven't heard of that!"

Vitamin N stands for *No*—not just the word but the concept. First-time parents fall into the trap of thinking that they can make their child happier and better adjusted by what they give to their child and the experiences they provide for their child. A lot of times, these efforts can backfire.

I don't want to pick on the Mouse too unfairly, but when you take your little kid to Disneyland at age three, buy him Mickey ears, a Goofy T-shirt, an Aladdin sword, Lion King pajamas, and Donald Duck sunglasses, and push your stroller the length of California, don't be surprised if, at midnight, you rub your sore feet, look at each other, and conclude that this may have been the worst day of your life.

Not giving your kids things is very important. Too often giving our children things becomes a substitute for being their parents. We haven't spent enough time at home, so we try to make up for it by taking our kids to Disneyland—which doesn't really give us time together as much as it diverts us from the real world.

This is a rut that parents can fall into for their entire lives. We want our kids to busy themselves as eight- to twelve-year-olds, so what do we do? We buy them videos and video games, buying time for ourselves but in the process alienating our family. The more things a kid has, the less time he usually spends with Mom and Dad.

Kids don't need half as much as we give them. I know a young father who was eager to give his firstborn everything she wanted. He and his wife were on a very tight budget, however, and could hardly afford anything. One Sunday they dropped their daughter off at the church nursery. When they picked her up an hour later, Dad noticed how much his little girl loved playing with a roly-poly chime ball. He went to the store and found it for twelve dollars. That may not sound like much to you or me, but they didn't have any slack in their budget. Without conferring with his wife, Dad bought the ball. He wanted his little girl to be happy.

84

Imagine his disappointment when he got home, took the chime ball out of the box, and placed it on the floor. His baby pushed past the chime ball and started playing with the box.

"No, honey!" he said. "Look at the ball! See how it jingles? It's just like the one you saw at church." But baby was transfixed by that box; she never even looked at the chime ball.

Most babies grow tired of toys after about five minutes. If you take your child to a friend's house and watch while they play with a friend's toy and then go out and buy it, thinking your child will have hours of fun with it, you're making a classic first-time parent mistake. Toys last about as long as leftovers. Babies lose interest faster than you can believe. So put your energy and finances into spending time with your baby and interacting with her rather than giving her things.

Look at it this way: *An unhappy child is a healthy child.* Did that statement surprise you? Children need to learn how to handle denial; they need to learn how to work through disappointment. What better place to do that than at home? And what better person to learn it from than their mother or father?

4. LACK OF VITAMIN *E*

One of the biggest myths today is the concern over self-esteem. Self-esteem, as it is commonly preached, is often nothing but blue smoke that you blow your kids' way; it's all the "Rah-rah, you're great this, you're great that, you truly are special" blather that "experts" suggest produces healthy kids.

The problem I have with this approach is that it's not tied to integrity, to character. Nor to the notion of giving back to the family. It's esteem built on an illusion! The thinking is that if you do all these wonderful things for your children and enrich their lives this way and that way, somehow this kid will be the most beautiful butterfly you've ever seen, totally in love with all the spots on her wings. The fact is, that kind of blue smoke lasts about as long as a fruit fly; it's not sustaining.

Instead of telling a child how wonderful she is just for being a child, you want to teach your child to think in a constructive, positive manner. Esteem comes from accomplishing something and from giving something back. If a kid earns something or learns how to do something, and her parents come alongside her and comment about what a great job she did or what a great effort she made or how good she must feel inside for what she has accomplished, that girl starts thinking to herself, *The most significant people in my life—my mommy and my daddy—notice what I've done and what I've accomplished and recognize that I have a role to play.* This is what builds esteem, because it's built on substance.

Listen—kids aren't as stupid as we think they are. When

85
• • • • •

you tell a kid how wonderful he is and he knows he's not wonderful, how do you think that settles in his mind? The only thing this tells him is that he can't trust Mom or Dad, so that when a genuine accomplishment deserves encouragement, he can't receive it. After all, he knows his parents lied to him before; how does he know they're not lying to him now?

One father laughed when his young daughter called one track meet's "participant" ribbons "Good job anyway" ribbons. She quickly grew tired of these meaningless strips, and rightly so. It's an accomplishment to finish a marathon; it's not a particular accomplishment for a ten-year-old to finish a fifty-meter dash (excepting Special Olympics, or something like that, of course).

This laissez-faire self-esteem guide to permissive parenting is based on feeling good. It empowers kids in all the wrong ways. Kids are hedonistic, and they'll work you if you fall into this trap. If you let them think for one minute that their happiness is your primary goal in life, they will pull on your heartstrings, play the sob-story violin for all it's worth, and end up as selfish adults who should be ashamed, not proud, of their self-centeredness. Your job is to make sure you're the parent, not some kind of chump for them to chew up and spit out.

Instead of focusing on your child's self-esteem, focus on raising a person who is a giver rather than a taker. One very practical way to do this is to teach your children to write thank-you notes. Even a birthday present from Grandma isn't a "right;" it's a privilege, and should be treated as such. Teaching kids to say "thank you" works against that "taker" mentality, as it's a form of "giving back."

Another approach Sande and I like to use is to involve our kids in acts of charity. If you know of a family who could use some extra grocery money, write a card, put the cash inside, and have one of your children walk it to the door. What this does is teach your kid that Mommy and Daddy are concerned about giving to others.

As a family, we sponsor a boy in El Salvador through Compassion International; Lauren loves to write letters to him. In addition to regular support, we like to get creative. One time I went to a flea market and purchased a bunch of baseball bats, baseball gloves, and numerous balls, enough for the whole neighborhood to play! Lauren was a part of finding and purchasing the equipment, as well as packing and mailing that package.

It comes down to this: If you want to raise a compassion-ate child, then give him something to be compassionate about. Your ultimate goal is to build a child who is independ-ent after college, able to succeed without Mom or Dad look-ing over his shoulder and constantly telling him how special he is for getting that C on his chemistry final.

Though I'm not big on filling a child's schedule with activi-ties, what I love about a club like 4-H is that a kid will take on a project—raising a calf, for instance—and learn to see the project through from square one. At the end, if they do a good job, they get the blue ribbon at the fair—and they've earned it! That sense of accomplishment and pride is a good thing because it's based on substantive reality. They didn't just try hard—they succeeded. In the real world, that's a significant difference and a very important distinction.

I know of a grown man who remembers talking to his dad after his team lost an important game. The son had made a couple of mistakes that he really shouldn't have made. The father didn't berate his son or chastise him for failing to be perfect, but he did say, "Son, I want you to remember how it feels to lose and never forget it. That's the motivation you need to try even harder next time." While this might sound harsh to some of you, consider, for a moment, how such a boy will respond when he gets turned down for his first job interview. Instead of crying about how the company couldn't see his "special" qualities, he'll have learned how to work harder to make himself that much more attractive for his next job interview—a very valuable lesson.

True encouragement means recognizing what a child does and acknowledging her actual accomplishments—whether those accomplishments take place in school or at home. It's about noticing those things that deserve to be noticed, and taking the time to mention them.

Here's an example from my own family. Not that long ago, Hannah and I had a talk. I told her how proud I was of the friends she was choosing. I pointed out the positive characteristics of these friends, and why I thought they were good companions, and I mentioned how pleased I was that Hannah was being so wise about the people she chose to spend her free time with. How did this make Hannah feel? It gave her a warm sense of accomplishment: *My dad is affirming my choices, which must mean I'm able to make wise choices.* Such comments to children will only increase their confidence and help them continue to make wise choices into the future.

This is how you build true, healthy esteem in children: Encourage their good thinking (vitamin E). Point out what they're doing right. Notice the choices and actions that are worthy of encouragement, and don't be sparing. But shelve the empty rah-rah, "you're special because you're you" stuff.

When you get down to it, the most important thing we teach our kids is about making the right choices, which is why I usually read the newspaper within earshot of my children. I read about negligent car accidents, college students poisoning themselves with alcohol, and we talk about it. "What do you think that kid was thinking?" I'll ask.

"That's the problem," one of my kids might say. "He wasn't thinking."

With a very young child, you have to take it down a notch. "Jeffrey, Mommy was really pleased when you shared your toys with Hannah today. That shows you're getting to be a big boy!"

Admittedly, this can get a little slippery. You need to come alongside of your child and encourage what he has done without (a) overdoing it and (b) communicating the untruth that Mom or Dad loves you because you did that. I'm not preaching conditional love here. I'm just saying that self-esteem is best built on substantive achievements, not empty platitudes.

Just about every activity in a kid's day affords you the opportunity to supplement your child's character with vitamin E. Let's take something as simple as teaching them to put away their toys. With an eight-year-old you can say, "Honey, I want you to pick up all these toys as soon as the *Gilligan's Island* rerun is over," and he should be able to do it. With a two-and-a-half-year-old, you can't simply say, "Pick up your toys." You have to physically get down on the floor with your child and help her put things away. You also have to have realistic expectations. Her idea of putting things away might be picking up the little plastic truck and dumping it in a box. To that, you might say something like, "Thank you for helping Mommy," maybe even clapping your hands together. In most cases a child this age will clap her hands together in response and smile. The takeaway, as simple as this sounds, is that the child thinks, *I can help Mommy. Mommy noticed me helping!* She is already being set up for the notion that she can give something back to her family. I can't

89

overstress how important this sense of esteem and family belonging will be once she reaches adolescence.

5. GETTING CAUGHT UP IN THE COMPETITION GAME

Are you raising the kind of baby who only wears the latest BabyGap clothes, Hannah Anderson outfits, or other expensive designer duds? Are you concerned that your child has the latest brain-stimulation toys, is developing physically faster than other kids her age, and is talking sooner as well?

I've met parents who look at educational toys designed for two- to three-year-olds and give them to their nine-month-old, then gush enthusiastically when that nine-month-old enjoys playing with them. "Look at that!" they say. "He's well advanced for his age! He's not supposed to be playing with it for another fifteen months!"

Try not to push your child. A nine-month-old can enjoy just about anything if her mother is gushing over her shoulder; it doesn't mean much. Besides, human development is a long process. Early development does not guarantee that a child will be above average her entire life; she may well be passed up by her peers by kindergarten or maybe not till high school. By the time we hit our twenties, a few of us are above average, a few are below average, and the vast majority are right in the middle. In the end, does it really matter all that much?

Avoid the "Well, my child" game like the plague. The "Well, my child" game goes like this:

> Mother number one: "My child said her first word at nine months!"
> Mother number two: "Well, my child took his first steps at eight and a half months!"

Mother number three: "All my children were potty
trained by eighteen months!"

Human development isn't a race; it's not who gets
anywhere first! Character takes seasoning and really isn't
seen until we're adults. I can probably drum up hundreds of
kids who rolled over onto their stomachs before all their
peers—and who ended up in jail. Don't worry about other
kids' progress compared to yours, and don't gloat if your
kid's progress seems advanced. It doesn't matter.

Be careful. Good motivation can create disastrous
parenting. If you are determined to be the perfect parent, the
kind who reads three different parenting magazines, all the
latest books, and charts your child's progress to the month,
taking everything personally (that's the key), your kid will
eventually use that against you. He will realize that you have
given him a great deal of power over you.

91

He may well bide his time until he turns eight or nine.
Maybe he'll wait until he's an adolescent to rebel. Maybe
he'll hold off until he goes away to college, but inevitably, a
child with even normal intelligence will pick up on your
tense motivation and think to himself, *Mom's really big on
this; I think I'll take this on as a personal agenda!* Kids have
an intuitive and pretty accurate understanding of what we
want them to do, and the strong-willed ones will really
give you a run for your money if they pick up on your motivation to be the perfect parent who is producing the perfect
kids.

Instead of comparing your kid, enjoy him. Like a hyacinth,
plant the seed, wait awhile, keep your eyes focused, enjoy
the first little sprout, and then let yourself be enamored with
the beauty of what ultimately comes out—twenty years
down the road.

You miss so much when you get caught up in the comparison game. Your firstborn will never be as little as she is now. I remember holding my fourthborn, Hannah, who weighed five pounds two ounces at birth. She fit in one hand, and I kept saying to myself, "I catch bass this big on a routine basis!"

Perhaps because I had already raised three children into near-adulthood by the time Hannah arrived, I was able to enjoy her all the way around. I loved her at five pounds; I got a kick out of her at twenty-five pounds. I never stopped adoring her even when she seemed stuck at sixty pounds for two years; and I love her now as she approaches 100 pounds.

When she gets married and is nine months pregnant, I'm sure I'll love her at 150 pounds!

Just yesterday (as I write this) the two of us were pretending that we were dancing at her wedding. Hannah might forget that moment, but I never will. I know how fast the days can race by, so I'm holding on to every memory and not letting a single one be stolen by comparing Hannah to her friends. Frankly, I don't care which friend is two inches taller, thirty seconds faster in the mile, or twenty points higher on the IQ test. Out of all the kids in the world, including famous pop stars, actresses, book authors, news anchors, you name it—I'd choose Holly, Krissy, Kevin, Hannah, and Lauren 100 times out of 100.

6. GETTING OVEREXCITED

I've flown millions of miles. That's not an exaggeration; on American Airlines alone, I've passed the three-million mark. I've flown through every type of turbulence and inconvenience you could imagine.

But I still remember the first time I went through turbulence. We got up in the air, the plane started to shake, and I started to panic. *What's going on?* I wondered. *What's happening?*

But then I looked around me. The man next to me kept reading his paper, as if nothing were happening. The woman across the aisle wasn't breaking a sweat. Seeing their calm helped me to be calm. I learned that turbulence is a normal part of airline travel, like occasional bumps in the road when you're driving; it's nothing to be frightened about.

Today I'll occasionally see some other rookies facing their first bout of turbulence. Anxiety takes over their face until they look around and see that everybody else is pretty calm. Then they calm down, too.

As a first-time parent, you'll go through many trials and anxieties for the first time. With child number two, you won't sweat these same trials quite so much because you've been through it before and learned that your baby will survive a rising temperature or an occasional bout of diarrhea.

But since (unlike being on a plane) as a first-time parent in your own home there is no one else to look to, your tendency is going to be to get a little too excited about minor things.

Why is this a problem?

Well, remember when we talked about bonding? I said that not only will you be able to read your child, your child will be able to read you. You won't be able to hide your anxiety from your baby, Mom—she knows you. When you hold her, she hears your heart beating 150 beats a minute and thinks, *What's up with this? Something must be wrong!* When your voice is strained or worried, she picks it up like a lie-detector test. Nothing passes by her because for several months, you've been her entire world. She has studied you and she knows you. She is the last person you can fool.

93
* * * * *

Babies do best with calm, confident mothers. It gives them a sense of security, serenity, and peace. Learn to speak soothing words instead of scooping up your child at the slightest whimper. Your baby will take her cues from you. If she hears you calmly speaking to her, she'll think, *Well, Mom's not upset; everything must be okay. Maybe I should settle down, too.*

What I see happen all too often with first-time mothers is that the baby gets agitated, which makes the mother get agitated, which makes the baby even more agitated, which, of course, makes the mother get more agitated, and on and on it goes.

Relax. Be calm. Present a soothing presence to your baby. Don't treat minor instances like they are life-and-death occurrences.

Another way that first-time moms get overexcited is by treating normal developments as if their child had surpassed Einstein. You won't do this with child number two or three, but I guarantee you're going to do it with child number one.

Let's talk about baby's first outside-the-diaper bowel movement, for instance. It's no secret that when you feed a child breast milk, Similac, or jars of baby food, it's eventually going to come out the other end. Happens all the time. In China. In Peru. In Yugoslavia. And yes, in the good old United States. Babies eat. Babies poop.

No big deal, right?

Well, it is to the firstborn's parents!

Twenty-month-old Frederick finally gets it and climbs up on the big toilet—not the little plastic potty chair, mind you, but the big potty that says Eljer on the back of it. After a minute or two of contemplation, he goes number two, and guess who happens to walk by? First-time Mom, that's who.

First-time Mom does a double take when she sees Frederick on the "big boy potty." Then she looks in the bowl and discovers that Frederick has created a four-and-a-half-inch masterpiece, floating peacefully in the toilet. Proud as a peacock, first-time Mom yells for her husband, "Harold, Harold, come here quickly! Come see what little Frederick has done!"

First-time Dad puts down the sports page, looks into the bowl, and says, "That a boy. Good boy. That's really good work there."

What is twenty-month-old Frederick thinking? *You know, that was pretty easy; one little grunt and there it was. These people will do anything for entertainment.*

If you overreact to the little things in life, you set yourself up for massive disappointment; you also risk giving your child a messiah complex. When you start overly worrying about the basics: child eating, child wetting and soiling, sleeping, etc., you're barking up a tree with not a raccoon in sight. Over a period of time, if you overreact to these natural things, the child is going to react back. Inwardly he'll think, *Oh, they're really big on that aren't they?* And then your child will use that new power against you.

If you overreact, you are taking normal things and turning them into power struggles. I've seen parents with Ph.D.s make fools of themselves with a child's spoon, trying to trick that child into eating: "Here's the plane, honey; open up wide for the plane!" As soon as the plane enters airspace directly in front of the kid's mouth, that kid's lips clench tightly shut. The hangar is closed!

Or first-time moms get uptight because their baby is crying. Babies are supposed to cry; that's what they do! You're a new mom, you've been hugging her and kissing her and singing to her all day long. Hey, treat me like that and I'm going to cry, too, when you leave me!

95
* * * * *

A bowel movement is not a great achievement. I found out as a little boy, experimenting with my sister Sally's dolls, that what goes in has to come out. I know, because I tried Pepsi, milk, iced tea (and a few other substances I'd prefer my mom not know about), and every one of them came out of the plastic body of Betsy the cry-and-poop doll.

So although it may be the first time for you, Mom, what is taking place happens every day and has for thousands of years.

7. OVERDISCIPLINE

As a first-time mother, you're probably not as familiar with age-appropriate behavior as a second- or third-time mother will be. Because of this, you're more likely to overdiscipline your child.

I hear the stories all the time: A three-year-old steals a cookie and then lies about it; first-time mom spanks the child, puts her to bed without dinner, and then treats her like a third-class citizen for four days. "Are you lying to Mommy again? Are you sure? Let me count the cookies one more time, because you know Mommy can't trust you anymore."

With very young kids it's far more beneficial to take the opportunity to train rather than to shame and shun. If my three-year-old stole a cookie and then lied about it, I'd simply take her aside and say, "Honey, listen, I happen to know that's not the truth. There were three cookies here just five minutes ago, and now there are only two. Nobody else has been here except for you and me. You took that cookie, didn't you?"

"Maybe."

"Honey, how would you feel if you asked me if we could go out for ice cream and I said yes, but when you came out of your bedroom with your shoes on, all ready to go, I said, 'I never told you we'd get any ice cream. Go back to your room and take your shoes off.' You wouldn't like that, would you?"

"No."

"You see honey, it's very important in a family for everyone to tell the truth. That way we can depend on each other. So let me ask you again: Did you take that cookie?"

"Yes."

Following this confession, you might want to withhold her dessert for lunch or dinner, but anything more than this is overkill. Don't turn a pimple into Mount Saint Helens!

97

Sometimes we forget that little kids are people; they're not robots. They get tired, and when they get tired, they get cranky. Sometimes their crankiness is our fault; we keep them out too late, we try to overdo it, and then we wonder why they're behaving so badly.

Quite often, it's best to simply put your child down for a nap when she's being irritable rather than trying to make a life lesson out of one impatient act. Learn to recognize your child's human limitations and stop expecting her to always respond with robotic regularity. Take the time to find out what's going on: "Are you frightened, honey? Is something hurting you? I bet you're really tired, aren't you?"

Too many first-time parents read into a kid's behavior things that just aren't true. A kid is tired, but the parent acts like that child is a criminal in the making. Instead, simply treat the tiredness, and the seeming rebellion will melt away—then you can deal with *real* rebellion when it arises.

I've even seen normal, healthy curiosity mistaken for

rebellion. One time, while hosting a radio talk show, I got a call from a mother of a nine-month-old.

"Dr. Leman," she said, "this morning my child was willfully disobedient, and I want to know how to make her learn to behave."

"What did she do?" I asked.

"She walked up to the couch and grabbed some decorative pillows. I told her not to throw them on the floor, but she looked me right in the eyes and did it anyway. These are beautiful, handmade pillows; they're very expensive."

I wanted to immediately lecture this mom on how little a nine-month-old cares about the cost or the manufacturing process of a pillow—but I held myself in check long enough to ask, "What did you do to her?"

"I smacked her a good one. She won't do that again!"

"How old did you say your child is?" I asked again.

"Nine months."

I was shocked. "Don't you understand that what that baby did was developmentally appropriate behavior? She's not defying you, not at that age. It was a neat game. She saw the colorful pillows, but she doesn't understand how one pillow costs two dollars and another costs fifty dollars; she just saw the decoration and thought it would be fun to see it drop."

Babies love cause and effect; they are just figuring out their world. Gravity, the way food feels in their hands or on their hair, the sound a cup of water makes when it falls on the floor, the way a dog yelps when his tail gets pulled—all that is new to them. Their lack of experience means they could care less if they're dropping Kmart value plates or your wedding china; it's all the same to them.

Read enough about kids to keep yourself from overreacting, like smacking a kid for doing something that's developmentally appropriate. Remember: Your goal is not to control the child; your goal is to be in authority in a healthy way. If all you do is control an easily controlled child, you're setting that child up to be easy prey in the adolescent years when peer pressure replaces parental influence.

I'm not suggesting that you be lackadaisical in your discipline, but don't put a tag of rebellion on every childish act or curiosity-induced experiment.

8. UNDERDISCIPLINE

NBA All-Star Jason Kidd plays with a flamboyant style. He finds and creates passing lanes that few could imagine, making him a fan favorite as well as a welcomed teammate for those who benefit from his passes.

But his story has its dark side. [3]

After five years of marriage, tension in the Kidd household had become pretty thick. On January 18, 2001, it exploded when Joumana (Jason's wife) told Jason not to pick at T. J.'s (their son's) food. Jason responded by spitting a French fry at her. Then he punched her in the face.

Joumana fled upstairs and locked herself in the bathroom. She called 911, then hung up. Following protocol, the 911 dispatchers called back, and Jason answered the phone. He handed it to Joumana, who told the dispatcher what happened. Later T. J. watched while the police took his dad away.

To his credit, Jason has worked hard at controlling his rage. He's been faithful in counseling. He told Joumana that calling the police was the right thing to do. His therapist says she has worked with athletes on about 200 cases of domestic violence, and not a single one has responded "as positively" as Kidd has.

99
* * * * *

But the damage was still done.

Sports Illustrated reporter S. L. Price observed how T. J. already imitates Jason's dribble and foul-line stance "with astonishing accuracy."

Unfortunately, that's not all he imitates.

Price watched as Jason was filming a commercial—a long, arduous, and usually boring task—and T. J. was running out of patience. Joumana was doing her best to keep T. J. from getting in the way, which would only delay the shoot and make them have to start all over again.

In a desperate attempt to distract her son, Joumana grabbed hold of him and asked, "Did you have a nice time at school?"

T. J. turned and hit her "square in the cheek" with his right hand.

Joumana simply grabbed his hand and repeated her question.

T. J. hit her again, then walked away. Instead of disciplining her son, Joumana rolled a ball his way. T. J. laughed, picked it up, and started dribbling it, just like his dad.

This story teaches the importance of two things. First, kids are watching, and they will imitate not just our good habits but also our bad ones. Second, mothers can't ignore such blatant disrespect.

Now that I've warned you not to overdiscipline your child, I want to provide a balance by urging you not to underdiscipline your child. There's a line between expecting perfection and letting your child do everything he wants without consequences; it's not always easy, but you need to find the patience to discipline consistently.

When kids go bad, I can usually point to one of two problems: They were overdisciplined by rigid parents, or they were allowed to run free. Both ends of the spectrum ruin character.

With firstborns in particular, you need to lay out exactly what the rules are, and you need to follow up. The rules should be fair and age appropriate (i.e., putting away a toy that she can't play with—for a day), and there should be consequences for breaking them. The reason this is so important for firstborns is that a firstborn doesn't have the benefit of older siblings; she can't watch and see what older brother Tommy does with his dirty laundry. You have to tell her.

Now, certainly, there's a difference between being specific and overdoing it. When your child asks you what time it is, refrain from offering a lecture on the history of the human clock, from the sundial forward. On the other hand, as I already said, with a firstborn you may have to say more than "around noon." Another way of putting this—to use clichés—is to major on the majors and don't sweat the minor stuff. A child dropping a pillow isn't a big deal; a three-year-old slapping his mother is a big deal and should be responded to rather than ignored.

101

9. LETTING OTHER PEOPLE RAISE YOUR CHILD

This is your child. Nobody else will love her like you do. She may not have come at a convenient time. Career-wise, she might represent a big hiccup to your advancement. You may not be financially ready. But she's here. What are you going to do about it?

It's not like you can put her on hold for five years until you're more financially secure and your vocation has calmed down a bit. Every second of their lives our children march ever farther down the road of independence—and they rarely go backward. A baby will stay in your arms all day long; a two-year-old will take only so much cuddle time before she wants down to run.

If you don't slow down for the first three years, guess what? The "wet cement" in your baby's life will have already begun to harden. In fact, the first five years will be the most important five years of your child's life, developmentally speaking. Are you willing to simply forfeit the first three of those years until you get your job in order? I hope not!

If there was another way, I'd happily tell you about it, but there isn't. The person who spends the most time with your child over the first five years is the person who will most influence his or her development. The surroundings your child grows up in will have a major impact on her values, beliefs, and attitudes. If you create a healthy, well-balanced environment around your firstborn, your child will probably have a healthy, well-balanced outlook on life.

That means you'll have to make some tough decisions— and some sacrifices. But they'll be worth it in the end. This subject is such an important one—and so heatedly discussed by first-time parents—that it deserves a chapter all its own (see chapter 6, "To Work or Not to Work").

Another way you might let someone else raise your child is to give in too easily to your parents' or your in-laws' advice. As a first-time mom, it may take you awhile to assume your role as a full-fledged adult, responsible for the decisions you make. But remember that you're no longer under your parents' authority. You have to do what *you* think is best—no matter what your parents or in-laws think (or what they say to your face or behind your back). You're the one in charge, so take control. No one knows your child better than you.

10. ALLOWING YOUR CHILD TO BE THE CENTER OF THE UNIVERSE

Up until age two, a kid's favorite word is *mine*. This is especially true of a firstborn, who rarely has to share anything. A young toddler is just starting to identify with himself and things around him, and he associates every person and every object in relation to himself. A person who treats him nicely is a nice person (until that person does something that displeases him). A toy that he wants is a toy that he should have, for no other reason than he wants it.

The smart mother will teach her child the importance of sharing and giving.

Hey, Mom, take a look around: What do you see at the supermarket or the mall? Do you see what I see? Do you see two-and-a-half-feet-tall kids making all kinds of demands upon adults? "No, I don't want Corn Flakes, I want Super Sugar Puffs!" As I look around, I see a lot of self-centered, hedonistic little kids with a one-way agenda: *It's all about me.*

Can you blame them? Think about what we read. *People, Self, US,* even *USA Today*'s Life section—they are full of stories about people who look at life and say, *It's all about me.* By our nature, we care about ourselves first. But isn't it nice to read about someone who gave sacrificially to someone else? Maybe a brother donated a kidney to his kid sister; maybe an inmate out on work release found a wallet with five hundred dollars in it—and returned it. How can we raise kids to be like that?

Fortunately, I think the me-first selfish thing has kind of run its course. Or at least we're finally waking up to the fact that other people matter; other people have needs and wants. This is a lesson that needs to be taught to very young children.

103
• • • • •

You need to be aware, however, that children under the age of two naturally go through a "mine" stage. Trying to force them out of this prematurely just isn't going to work. I was in a restaurant recently, and a mom and her eighteen-month-old were sitting right behind me. In addition to the eighteen-month-old, the mother had an infant with her. For some reason the mother insisted on making the eighteen-month-old share his book with the baby, who obviously couldn't read it. That just made the eighteen-month-old scream all the louder: "My book, my book, mmmmyyyyy booooook!"

While I was sympathetic and even supportive of her desire to raise a child who would learn to share, I wanted to turn around and tell her that her kid was going through a stage of psychological and social development that you find in every child. Her insistence on him sharing his book with a little sister who can't read or even enjoy it is not only an effort in futility but one that won't help her child one iota.

You can't force every lesson—even the most important ones. As that boy gets closer to three years of age, then he'll become better at sharing, provided you haven't driven him to resent the process before then! Sharing is something you teach by demonstrating. You let Jeffrey have something of yours and say, "See, Jeffrey, Mommy shares with you, Daddy shares with you, Grandpa and Grandma share with you. Sometimes you need to share with baby Abigail."

As a kid grows from three to four, get more aggressive in this regard: Help your firstborn develop self-discipline, waiting her turn, not barging ahead in ice cream cone lines: "Honey, we need to wait. See the other people in front of us? That little boy will get his ice cream, then that little girl will get her ice cream, and then that Daddy with his two kids will get their ice cream, and then we'll be next. So what we need to think about now is, what kind will you want when you get up front?" You have to teach kids to become aware of others and not just selfishly barge ahead.

That's why if your child is the only child in the family, you may find preschool helpful for this reason: When a child hits age three, she needs to be taught how to share and take turns and compete and work with others. If your child doesn't have siblings, preschool is a good place to learn these lessons. If your child doesn't go to preschool, make sure you schedule playtimes where she can interact with a variety of other kids—and that you don't always come to her rescue before she has time to work out her own interactions with others.

105

ROUNDING THE CORNERS

These ten mistakes all center around the most likely character deficiencies of a firstborn. You can raise a leader or a tyrant, depending on whether she learns to be selfless or selfish. You can raise an influencer or a juvenile delinquent, depending on whether your firstborn is over- or under-disciplined, or disciplined just right. You can create an accomplished firstborn or a resentful firstborn, depending on whether you have a critical eye or whether you provide a healthy dose of Vitamin E.

So accept the unique qualities of your firstborn, embrace the tendencies that firstborns develop due to their role in the family tree, but then round the roughest corners. Take the sharp edges off. She's already programmed to succeed. Your job is just to point her in the right direction.

The Ten Most Common
First-Time Parenting Mistakes

1. A Critical Eye
2. Overcommitment
3. Not Enough Vitamin N
4. Lack of Vitamin E
5. Getting Caught Up in the Competition Game
6. Getting Overexcited
7. Overdiscipline
8. Underdiscipline
9. Letting Other People Raise Your Child
10. Allowing Your Child to Be the Center of the Universe

6

To Work or Not to Work
(outside the home)?

Not long ago, while killing time in the Atlanta airport, waiting for my flight to Buffalo, New York, I sat down next to a poster-material blonde baby and her very Italian-looking mother.

The mother shifted nervously when she saw me. No doubt she was thinking, *Oh, no. Now I've got to keep my baby especially quiet. This guy's old enough to be a grandpa, but what if he isn't? I wonder how patient he is. What if this kid starts to fuss?*

To set the mother at ease right away, I said with a grin, "Lucky me. I get to sit next to such a cute baby. She's adorable! I love babies! I've had five myself. And now the youngest is eleven, and the oldest is thirty. Time sure does fly."

The mother visibly relaxed and smiled.

In the course of our conversation over the next twenty minutes, before the boarding call was announced, the mother confessed, "I didn't really want to have any kids. And I certainly wasn't ready to stay home with them. My career was going really well. Then Anne came along"—she gestured toward her daughter—"and, well, I fell in love. With my daughter. And suddenly the choice that I had been wrestling over since the time I found out I was pregnant—to work, or not to work—wasn't so difficult anymore."

Women of the twenty-first century, you have choices. You are doing far more than any other generation of women ever did. For example, the very plane I took back to Buffalo was piloted by two people—and one of them was female. Previous generations of women wouldn't have dreamed of such a career opportunity.

Perhaps that's why it's so difficult for mothers today, as they wrestle with their own decision of whether to work at an "outside-the-home" career or not. Mothers today have all kinds of choices, and these choices can be exhausting. Just consider a few of them:

- I could work full-time in the office.
- I could work full-time from home.
- I could work part-time from the office, part-time from home.
- Maybe I could just work a few hours a week.
- I could put my career on hold for a few years and go back part-time when my child is in kindergarten.
- I could be a stay-at-home mom.

Since the options may be swirling in front of you, I'm dedicating this chapter to the most important decision you'll ever make in your child's first year: Who is going to raise her?

MEMORIES FOR A LIFETIME

If you've ever played golf, you can relate to those few times when everything went right as you drove the ball off the tee. When you finally reached your ball, well down the fairway, you looked back and thought, *Did I really hit it that far?* You look back and try to remember what it was that got you there so that you can do it again on the next hole.

Looking back at life can be a pretty good guide to what the future will bring, so I want you to take a quick journey through your own childhood. Take a moment right now to pause and think about some of your best memories when you were a little boy or girl. What comes to mind?

Some of my best memories include playing outside on a cold November day in Buffalo, New York, throwing rocks into the neighbor's goldfish pond, or playing with my trucks, moving sand around in the sandbox. But you know an even better memory? Hearing my mother call me in for lunch and serving me warm tomato soup with cheese sandwiches. Mom always put butter on the top of my tomato soup—I can still visualize that creamy butter spreading out and covering my soup. I just loved the way it tasted!

One day Mom seemed a bit rushed, so she asked me if I thought I could make my own soup and sandwiches. I told her with a straight face, "Well, I suppose I could, but it sure tastes better when you make it, Mom."

That's all she needed to hear. She set aside what she was doing and made me a lunch I'll never forget.

Think about what I just said. As a guy in his fifties, I've eaten well over 75,000 lunches in my lifetime. How many of those can I remember? Not very many. Tens of thousands of lunches have been lost and I'll never be able to recall them. So why do I remember this one lunch in particular, eating that tomato soup with the melted butter on top?

I remember it because it has very warm feelings connected with my mom.

Okay, still with me? Good. Someday, that child you're holding is going to be in his fifties, just like I am now. That may seem like a long time away, but it'll get here sooner than

109
* * * * *

you think. When someone asks him to remember something about his childhood, will he talk about the childcare worker who bandaged his knee? Will he make jokes about the institutional lunches he had while being raised in daycare? Will he talk about being tied into a line as he and fifteen other two-year-olds walked to the park with the worker-of-the-month?

Or will he talk about autumn afternoons and drinking a cup of hot chocolate while Mommy read him his favorite book? Will he laugh about the wagon rides you gave him on the way to the grocery store to pick up a gallon of milk? Will he remember the way you smelled as you hugged him close when he fell off his bicycle, and then gently washed his knee and put on a Sesame Street bandage?

The decision you make in the coming weeks will determine exactly what kind of memories your little boy or girl will have fifty years from now. It will also play a big role in determining what kind of mom or dad *your child* will become someday. As you make this decision, I want to challenge you to get in touch with the comfort-type feelings *you* had as a kid. Examine several of them closely, and I bet you'll find each particular feeling associated with an event that happened with a parent.

If you grew up in a healthy home, you know you were loved and you realize that your parents made a lot of sacrifices on your behalf. Some sacrifices were little—Dad putting down the paper to teach you how to throw a baseball; Mom letting you "help" her bake some cookies, even though she knew it would take twice as long doing it *with* you instead of *for* you. Other sacrifices may have been more significant: Dad taking on a second job; Mom going without stylish clothes so she could save some money for your clothes; driving the family vehicle until it gets close to 200,000 miles before buying another used one.

SACRIFICE—IT'S NOT A DIRTY WORD

If I was writing this book a generation ago, I could assume so much more. There was a time when parents expected to make sacrifices on behalf of their children. Though their standard of living was often less than it is today, they still welcomed a greater number of kids into their house. Times have indeed changed. Parents used to have lots of kids; today, kids have lots of parents—and those parents have even less time.

A 1999 Council of Economic Advisors report found that American parents have twenty-two fewer hours per week to spend at home, as compared with the average in 1969. Harvard sociologist Robert Putnam estimates that "families have meals together about one-third less often today than they did in the mid 1970s." He also believes that "parents are about one-third less likely to take vacations, watch television, or even chat with their children."[4]

Is this a trend you want to continue? Or is it something you'd like to fight against? When you choose to become a parent, you are also choosing to make sacrifices. By bringing a new person into your family, you have accepted an awesome responsibility. And that means that your time, your energy, and your priorities are no longer just centered around you. For some, that's a difficult transition. But remember this key fact: *Nobody can raise your child like you can.* You can make some sacrifices now that will make a tremendous difference in your child's life, beginning with making sure that if you are married, either you or your spouse stays home with your child full-time.

Yes, I know you graduated in the top 10 percent of your class—and that you're smarter than most of the men you've ever met. You may even have a master's degree or more.

But I'm still asking either you or your husband to put your career on hold. If your husband wants to stay home and he has the temperament to deal with colic, runny noses, and changing diapers, so be it. I don't care which parent stays home, but I think one needs to. Before you roll your eyes and call me unrealistic or figure that I grew up in the Dark Ages, hear me out. And then you can decide for yourself.

A recent study out of Columbia University found that children whose mothers took jobs working thirty hours per week or more before the child was nine months old scored lower in both mental and verbal development tests. The effect was greater for boys than for girls.[5] And those aren't the only detrimental effects. We try to kid ourselves that having our children away from us for a major portion of their day won't really affect them, but it does—intellectually, emotionally, relationally, and spiritually.

Just step back a minute and think about the awesome responsibility that almighty God has given you. Your child isn't an accessory to your life. You haven't bought the satellite-dish program with the NFL package on it; this is your child. The decisions you make about who takes care of this child will literally help shape another human being. Why wouldn't you want to do all you can to leave a positive imprint on your child's life? Once again speaking as a psychologist, I assure you that you can't do this from a distance, nor can you do it part-time. A child deserves full-time care from at least one parent—if at all possible.

BUT WHAT ABOUT THE BILLS?

Every place I go, women tell me, "You don't understand, Dr. Leman. I need to work."

The problem I have is with the word *need*. So often *need*

means wanting to drive a certain model of car, to live in a certain neighborhood, and to take vacations to exotic locations. It also often means "with the extra money we'll be able to provide more opportunities for our children."

Like what? Getting your child into the rat race of life more quickly by signing him up for every available program so he won't "miss out"?

I've heard many couples insist that both husband and wife must work full-time, and I suppose that in rare circumstances this could be true. But all too often, I don't think it is. In more cases than otherwise, both spouses work simply to add to their possessions. If you're a single parent, you probably do need to work—but the important questions you have to ask yourself are similar: *How much am I working? Is it to provide for our real needs, or simply to add to my possessions or to ensure all the "right" opportunities for my child?*

When you're willing to sacrifice, you'll learn how to do without some privileges and quite a few extra possessions. When Holly was born, Sande and I owned just one car. Both of us grew up in a two-car family, and everybody we knew owned two cars, but we couldn't afford it because we had both agreed on Sande staying home with the kids. How did we decide? We asked ourselves similar questions to the ones I'll be sharing with you later in this chapter.

Because of these years, I know the fear of living with expenses that always seem greater than income. I am not unsympathetic to, or unfamiliar with, real financial need. I know exactly what it feels like to have to choose between buying milk or laundry detergent on any given shopping trip.

People look at me now as a best-selling author with two homes, but it wasn't always this way. And certainly not when the first three children were very young. In 1981, before I started publishing books and had my own counseling practice, I made just $22,000 a year. We had three children back then, by the way. When we got a letter announcing that the mortgage payment on our house was going up from $188 to $212 a month, I just about died. I can still remember holding that letter in my hand thinking, *How are we going to handle this?* Surprising as it may seem, I honestly had no idea how we'd come up with another $24 a month, but we did what any number of parents have done—we scrimped and cut and made sacrifices.

But never did we question our decision to keep Sande home. When we first got married, Sande worked as a service rep for Ma Bell; she quit when Holly was born. Once the kids were in school, Sande became a preschool teacher so she could be home when the kids got home and still help out with our family income.

There were many humbling moments in those years. We didn't buy many clothes but gratefully accepted the hand-me-downs that had a way of showing up on our door-step or in our living room. Our big treat out was to go to a cafeteria where our family of five ate for less than $15.

Because we had just one car and I had to drive it to work, Sande's big outing was when my dad would pick her and the kids up and take them to Sambo's restaurant, home of the ten-cent cup of coffee.

It was a sacrifice, but we got through it. And you know what? We wouldn't change a thing. As crazy as this may sound, sometimes I have a certain nostalgia for those years, just scraping by, trusting God, feeling so pleased knowing that Sande was home with the kids. It reminds me of that old Johnny Mathis song, "The Hungry Years," when he sings about how he misses them.

Here's another side you often don't hear: Th
had to sacrifice for a good decade to make our
come true of having Sande stay home with t⎰
have now enjoyed three decades of being very ∪.
family. My friend Moonhead (yes, I know, what a nam⎰
laughs at the way my family members blubber with each
other whenever one of us is going to be gone for any period
of time. We're looking forward to several more decades of
being part of a family that wants to stay together, even as
adults.

So you tell me: Was one decade of sacrifice worth five or
six decades of being part of a very special and close family?

Do you think our kids would still want to get together if
home life had been rushed, harried, and so broken up with
multiple activities that we barely had time to get to know
one another? The last thing a working mom has in the morning is unhurried time, and the last thing she has in the evening
is energy. As a result, baby usually gets shortchanged on
both ends.

Do you think our children would think of home as such a
warm place if they had been raised with continual daycare?
I may sound hard-core on this, but a lifetime of counseling
families has convinced me that they wouldn't.

Sande and I may have made many sacrifices, but we are
reaping the rewards of those sacrifices every day now that
three of our children are adults.

FACTORS TO CONSIDER

Although you already know what Sande and I chose to do
about her working when our children were young, every
family needs to make the decision about "To Work or Not to
Work" for themselves. That's because every family has a

different dynamic—due to differing personalities, energy levels, and income levels, to name a few issues.

As you are making your decision, prayerfully consider these factors:

Realize your own energy level.

Let's face it. Some people have more energy than others. They require less sleep. They are able to juggle more activities and more people with less stress than others. Becoming a mom will be one of the most stressful, time-consuming responsibilities you will ever have. If working full-time or part-time exhausts you now, and you have a hard time juggling other life tasks (doing laundry, cooking meals, getting your Round Tuits done) *now*, realize it's going to get much harder with a child. Not to mention the fact that you'll have more to do with lots of sleep interruptions and you may not be in top form physically, mentally, or emotionally.

Adjust for the age, stage, needs, and personality of your particular child.

Whether you work outside the home or not (or even freelance, inside the home) may vary, depending on your child's age. For instance, it may be easier to fit a few hours in when your child takes two naps a day. When your child takes only one, and then drops that nap, work hours for anything but tending to home and the child may be few and far between. It may be easier to work ten to fifteen hours a week when your child is in kindergarten for two to three hours a day, five days a week.

Also, some children just need more continual interaction than others. You may have a daughter who will sit by your side, at her own little desk, and happily color while you get an hour's worth of work done at the computer. Your neigh-

bor may have a daughter who can't sit still for more than five
minutes without parental interaction and suggestions of new
activities. Some children adapt easily to a lot of flurry and
noise, so being with other children in a group setting is enjoyable to them. Other children, more introspective by nature,
may not get the quiet time they need to thrive emotionally
when they are constantly with other children.

Only you can judge the age, stage, needs, and personality
of your particular child. Just remember—what you decide
now may not work in a year. You need to be flexible and
adaptable, watching carefully to evaluate what your child
needs and when he needs it. That means you need to be a
student of your child—to *know* him intimately.

117

Figure out your *real* motivation for wanting to work.

If you're considering going back to, or staying in your career
full-time, part-time, or at least keeping up some hours in
order to stay in the field, ask yourself some honest questions:
Are you considering working because of bills or health insur-
ance? Do you feel you need a job in order to "be" someone?
to show your worth? to hold your position of power in the
family? to prove that you *can* earn income, and thus are valuable?

Being aware of your own hidden motivations can help you
make a solid decision—and one that will be healthy for your
child as well.

Don't forget that, contrary to some people's opinions,
being a mother is already a full-time job—and it's a real job,
one of the busiest jobs in the world. From what other job do
you never get a vacation? No, you don't get a paycheck each
week. But the rewards are far more long lasting than dollar
bills in your hands.

Be aware of the overt costs of full-time or part-time childcare outside the home.

Many assume that working will always be financially benefi-cial to the family. But consider carefully the costs of childcare. If your child is in a continual daycare setting, such as at a daycare center or even in a private home, you'll usually pay a flat rate per week, or a certain amount of dollars per hour. One mom told me, "In the Chicago area, it costs me $8 an hour for childcare at my friend's house. That means it costs me $64 for a full day in the office. If I make $15 an hour, that basically means I'm working for $7 an hour, minus the gas and time it takes to get my child back and forth to my friend's. I've had to ask myself, *Is that worth it? To be away from my child for a whole day for only making about $5 an hour, by the time I count transportation costs and lunch out?*"

Many childcare systems are set up so that even if you decide to take off work for the day to do something fun with your child, you have to pay for that day anyway. (It guaran-tees the child a spot at that location.) So you don't have as much flexibility as you may think to pop in and out of childcare situations. Also, there may be additional fees for taking children to the zoo or the children's museum, for instance.

So evaluate carefully what you're *really* making financially, once you pay for childcare.

Recognize the hidden costs of working outside the home.

This is one area that lots of working folks miss. When you work outside the home (whether part-time or full-time), many times you have to keep up with a professional ward-robe, even if you are in the office for only a few hours. If you

118

were at home with the children, you might be able to buy ten "at-home" casual outfits for what it would cost for one professional outfit.

Also, will you spend more on groceries, buying the "quick fix" type of meals, rather than cooking from scratch? Or will your meals tend to be a lot more take-out food or restaurant visits than you'd make if you were a stay-at-home parent?

How much money will you spend in transportation to and from your job, and from the place where your child will be during the day?

Look for the type of environment your particular child will feel safe in.

Again, it goes back to your child's temperament. There are a lot of options—to stay at home full-time with your child, to use daycare part-time or full-time, to use Grandma or Grandpa as a part-time baby-sitter, to job share, to use a church-run childcare. The possibilities and combinations of them are seemingly endless, but *you* are the one who needs to choose what's best for your child. After all, you're the one responsible for her "all-day care."

DAYCARE OPTIONS

Always remember that you have options—and that you don't have to do things "like everybody else." After examining the factors above, if you still are in a position where you need to explore care for your child outside of yourself or your spouse, think carefully through the type of environment your particular child will feel safe in.

Sometimes daycare really is a must. You might be a single mom and really have no alternative. Or your husband might be too ill to watch the kids or work, and your family needs an income. You may be buried in debt, and you may be forced

119
• • • • •

to work your way out of it. Some of you are in those types of situations. That's why this chapter isn't meant to make you feel guilty but to give you practical information that can still help you make the best decision for your family, given the circumstances.

Consider a family member or close friend.

If you come from a healthy family and you're close enough to live near Grandpa and Grandma, take advantage of that. No, they may not promise to provide "intellectual stimulation" or painting or number-and-letter games, etc., but they provide several major benefits. First, it's likely they already love your child—and any child will respond to the safety and warmth of such love. Second, they know your child, and your child knows them, so your child is less likely to feel that "separation anxiety" from you. Third, they will most likely stick around. They're not minimum-wage workers who will leave as soon as somebody offers an extra seventy-cents an hour to work somewhere else. Staying with grandparents also opens up a whole new avenue of learning—like learning how to make melt-in-your-mouth peanut butter cookies and discovering the very happy fact that while Mom allows just one treat a day, Grandma and Grandpa's limit is thirteen.

Even better: See if Grandma and Grandpa can come to your home. If they can't come to your home every day you need childcare, ask them to come a day or two a week. Then your child has the added benefit of being home, his favorite place.

If grandparents aren't available, maybe you have a sibling who stays home with her child and would charge you just a small fee to have your child stay with her. If you don't have any relatives in this situation, maybe you have a close friend.

My point is that a relative or friend—and preferably another parent—will offer better emotional care than a paid stranger.

What about "at home" childcare?

Some parents who want to stay home with their children and need income decide to run an "at home" childcare, with perhaps four or five children other than their own in their care. A good way to investigate such a possibility is through your local church or your "friends network." It's even better if you know the parent running such a service. But if you don't, phone the person. Even if she's highly recommended by someone you know, arrange a visit to her home—during the day, while she has children there. See the types of activities she does with them, examine her playroom, ask how she handles discipline, how she handles "days off" and vacation season. Find out how many children she has at one time—and the age ranges of them. And make sure that she's licensed in childcare. (If you want to handle childcare costs through FlexComp, the childcare worker has to be licensed.)

121

Check out a church-run facility.

If you are involved with a church that has such a childcare program, it would be worth checking it out. Oftentimes church-run facilities will hire staff members who have more of a sense of "ministry"—or at least volunteers who volunteer their time because they really care about seeing children develop emotionally, relationally, physically, and spiritually. So go for a visit. Take your child with you to see how the child interacts with other children and the adult workers there. Ask similar questions to the ones you'd ask a "stay-at-home" childcare person.

Observe daycare centers in person.

If you absolutely must place your child in a daycare center, choose the place carefully. Money shouldn't be your primary concern; you may have to sacrifice to come up with another $100 a month, but it will be worth it to make sure your child is in the best place possible.

Do your research carefully and get several options. Then take a tour of the facilities. As you walk around, ask yourself, *Is this a place I'd like to go to if I were a little kid? Do the adults seem to genuinely care about the kids?* To find out about this, you're going to need to visit during regular hours, and you should plan to stay at least a couple hours. Remember, you're not choosing a mechanic; you're placing your child in another person's care—not just for a half hour, but for the best hours of her life, five days a week. Any group of workers can present a good front for twenty minutes, but it's going to be hard for them not to reveal what's going on if your stay is measured in hours.

Daycare centers remind me of a chicken farm I once visited. Rhode Island Red chickens lay eggs really well. Farmers keep them in these little white cubicles, and each hen's job is to produce an egg or two a day. Keeping everybody in individual cubicles is fine if your goal is to produce an egg, but it's not a good environment if your goal is to produce a compassionate and productive human being. Do I say this to make you feel horrible if your child is currently in a daycare center? No. But facts are facts: You can't fake a mother's concern. There is no way a daycare worker with twenty to thirty kids under her charge can mimic a mothering experience, regardless of how much she is paid. So to expect such centers to do so is to be entirely unrealistic. Unfortunately, being stuck in a room with fifteen other toddlers eight hours a day is not a healthy environment, nor is it well-balanced.

Just think about the people who usually work in daycare centers. All kinds of research shows that the turnover rate is appallingly high at most daycares because the pay most often is minimum wage. That means kids have to get used to the caregiver of the month as the daycare works feverishly to hire another worker—who, more often than not, has quite a low education, or she wouldn't accept the substandard wages that most daycares offer (see Dr. Brenda Hunter's book *Home by Choice*).

My rule of thumb is this: If you don't want your child to talk a certain way, then don't leave them with someone who talks that way for eight hours a day, five days a week.

Here's a quick list of things to consider (in addition to the questions already asked earlier in this section about other types of childcare), if you're questioning whether or not a daycare center is the right place for your child:

#1: *How healthy is the place?*

Are the facilities clean? How do the bathrooms look? Do toys that get put into other kids' mouths get washed, or are they just thrown back into the pile? Check out the diaper-changing station. Are workers washing their hands before they move on? Is the table cleaned between each diaper change?

#2: *What's the turnover rate of personnel?*

Don't allow staff workers to respond with general answers such as "pretty good" or "above average." I recommend that parents go to the individual workers, make pleasant small talk, and then ask, "How long have you been here?" If most of them have been there less than two years, you have your answer: Turnover is very high.

Listen to the workers talk: Your children will mimic their speech patterns. Are you okay with that? In her wonderful book *Home by Choice*, Dr. Brenda Hunter challenges and

123

enlightens readers by reminding us that the person who teaches a child to talk is the same person who teaches the child to think. Given such enormous influence, you need to be very confident of the person who will become your child's primary caregiver.

#3: *How does the staff handle discipline?*

As you look around and evaluate, ask yourself honestly: Are these the type of people you trust to discipline your children? What kind of discipline do you see happening around you? Is it the type of discipline you're comfortable with?

"Oh, but Dr. Leman, we wouldn't let our daycare discipline our kids!"

I understand that sentiment completely; I wouldn't want a stranger disciplining my kids either. But consider this: Do you think your child can go seven or eight or nine hours a day without being disciplined? I've never met a two-year-old who could!

TOUGH CHOICES

It comes down to this: I am asking you to make all kinds of sacrifices for your children. I realize that the word *sacrifice* is about as popular as the word *doormat* in our society, but I'd like to contend again, as I have earlier, that sacrifice is at the heart of parenting. I've never met a good, selfish parent.

Never.

"But Dr. Leman, all our friends have their kids in daycare."

Do you really want your family to look like everybody else's? That's not the goal I have for my kids, and I hope it's not the goal you have for yours, either.

Take it from a shrink who gets paid over $125 an hour to help people deal with unruly children: It's ultimately cheaper to make an investment of time, love, and sacrifice in the first

five to six years of your child's life than it is to cut corners
and have to pay the price later on. If you make shortcuts,
you're likely to either end up in some counselor's office,
hoping he can "cure" your child, crying because you and
your teen are so distant emotionally and can't understand
each other, or having to take out a loan to pay for acts of
vandalism, bail, or other teenage shenanigans. At twenty-
and-a-half inches, your baby may seem incapable of causing
trouble, but every single juvenile delinquent starts out as a
cute, cuddly baby. Just give him food, water, a lack of parental attention, and sixteen years to grow, and you'll be
amazed at the trouble he can cause.

So practice getting creative! Maybe you can find a job that
allows you to work part-time as opposed to full-time, juggling
your schedule with your husband's or another single parent's
so you can cut down on the amount of time your child is in
daycare. Don't expect these opportunities to fall into your
lap; you're going to have to go out there and search for
them. Pray about it. Talk to everyone you know. Be aggressive, because you'll never have a more important agenda to
fulfill.

What I'm talking about now has a name—*job sequencing*—
and it was practiced by none other than U.S. Supreme Court
justice Sandra Day O'Connor, who briefly left practice,
returned after caring for her young children, and still
managed to rise to the very top of her profession. A lot of
people are following O'Connor's lead and are undertaking
job sequencing today. The ones I've talked to are very happy
with their choice. One woman told me, "I know I could have
gone much further in my career if I didn't drop out for a bit,
but my kids will never say they felt shortchanged. I priori-
tized my life and put my family at the top of the list. Don't
get me wrong—I thoroughly enjoyed the vocational chal-

125
• • • • •

lenge, but the choice I made to stay home for a while reflects what I believe in, and I think that's what's important."

I give a woman like that a lot of credit. Mothers of today have all kinds of choices. Making the tough choice now is good practice for the future, because as a parent you'll be making tough choices for the next two or three decades. We had three kids in college at one time. If you think BabyGap clothes are expensive, try tuition (one of our kids went to a very expensive art school). Just think—you have all that still to look forward to!

IT'S ALL ABOUT THE FUTURE

More recently Sande has made a long-time dream come true by opening a funky, "shabby-chic" home décor store called The Shabbie Hattie. It takes a lot of work to get something like that going, and Sande put it off when the older kids needed her attention. But we still have a teen and a preteen at home, so Sande and I had a recent conversation about her leaving the store by 2:15 so she can pick up one of the kids while I get the other one. Two-fifteen sounds ridiculously early to leave a store that you're managing, but I reminded Sande that she needs a little kick-back time before the dinner hour. Our family holds dinnertime as sacred. It's the one time of the day when we're all together for the longest stretch, so we don't take it lightly.

Is this a sacrifice? You bet it is, but there are great rewards. Not that long ago, an editor came out to Tucson to go over a manuscript with me. Sande invited him to dinner, and all the kids were there, as well as my son-in-law. The next several times we spoke, that editor raved about the dinner, how much he enjoyed himself, and how impressed he was with our family's joy at just being together. What he couldn't see is that this happens all the time at our house; it wasn't particularly special. Our kids really enjoy being together. And we are humbly amazed.

Yes, sacrifices sting in the short-term, but in the long-term they pay great rewards.

Having one parent stay home or juggling your work schedule or number of hours might be a tough decision, but parenting is a grown-up task, and it will call you to make many tough decisions throughout the next two decades. Some years ago, Sande and I made a tough decision to take our kids out of public school. We felt it was important for them to receive a Christian education, where everything is taught in relation to the Christian faith. Private schools cost a good chunk of change, and back in those days, when we made the switch from public to private school, we used to polish every quarter that came through the door before we spent it.

But keep in mind—what seems like a sacrifice now may not seem like such a sacrifice if you just try it.

I know a mom who was very successful in her business. A top account executive making $70,000 a year, she always pictured herself being a career woman. She has an MBA degree, loves business, loves making the sale, and she gladly accepted the four months' maternity leave that her company gave her (which is about ten times longer than most new moms get).

But a funny thing happened on her way back to work: She fell in love with her son.

"I couldn't imagine missing a day of this wonderful gift of life, so I made the tough decision," she told me.

An even tougher decision was trying to figure out how to tell her husband about it. "He just about died when I told him what I was thinking," she admits. "He really couldn't believe

127

it because he always saw me as this corporate woman. And, of course, the first thing he saw was $70,000 going out the window. He even said, 'I guess we might as well kiss the new BMW good-bye and start looking for a minivan.'"

I admire this woman's spunk. She told me outright, "I'm the mom, and I don't want to miss a day of my son's life. I certainly don't want to put my son in the hands of a woman earning minimum wage who will be gone in three to six months and never think about him again."

Though this woman made a very courageous decision, there won't be any standing ovations over the choice she has made. Her choice won't result in a *Business Weekly* profile. She won't have the esteem of being given a promotion or a pay hike. Her IRA is going to take a real beating. And the main person who benefits from all this sacrifice—her son—doesn't even realize she's making a sacrifice. But she is determined that no one else is going to raise her child but her.

Are there some moms who have to work? Yes—and you may be one of them. Especially if you are the only wage earner—or the primary wage earner of the family. But just remember: You are a woman of choices. You can always get creative so that your child has as much "at home" time as possible. Plenty of jobs offer split schedules, or working-at-home flexibility. So don't sell yourself—or your child—out too easily without prayerfully considering all the options.

7

Caring for Your "Other Child"

If you're married, you've probably come to realize that you actually have more than one child living with you right now. There's the twenty-and-a-half-inch baby who sleeps in the crib, and then there's the five-foot-eleven-inch kid who sleeps in your bed.

At just the time most women want their husbands to act more like a man than ever before—to provide, offer strength, comfort, take charge, be selfless, sacrifice—they often find just the opposite: that hubby is acting more like a child than he ever has. (And guys, if you're reading this, don't go away mad. Read on—if for nothing else than to challenge my words and prove me wrong—and see if anything here could possibly sound like you.)

WHAT'S GOING ON HERE?

Take it from a psychologist: This is a very common and normal process for men to go through. Your husband isn't unusual if he's exhibiting this behavior, even seeming to be jealous of your baby. It happens all the time.

From your husband's perspective, the thing he liked most about marriage—having you all to himself, whenever he wants you—has suddenly been whisked away. Dinners are an afterthought. Sex has been radically altered. It takes more than a little creativity to have sexual relations with a woman in her third trimester, and then after birth, sex stops altogether while the wife heals. And once the wife's body does heal, husband soon finds out that her energy is depleted, and that a breast-feeding, diaper-changing mom doesn't smell like Chanel #5 anymore. For those of you with "chosen" children, you're adjusting to instant parenthood and the same energy depletion, not to mention the "baby smells" that would have gagged you previously.

Here's a little secret: Even your husband is frustrated with himself for feeling this way. He can't believe he's so petty that he's actually jealous of the time and energy you're putting into the child. He's as surprised by the fact that he has these feelings as you are appalled by the fact that he has them.

But there they are.

What are you two going to do about it?

MARRIAGES CAN'T HOLD THEIR BREATH

I want you to do something for me. Before you read any further, hold your breath for five seconds. Just five seconds, that's all I'm asking. Ready? Go.

Okay, some of you are cheating. Come on, it's just five seconds! Humor me! I'm giving you one more chance: Hold your breath till the count of five.

Good. All but the most stubborn of you are cooperating with my illustration. Now I want you to hold your breath for five minutes.

Ready, go!

What happened? How come you didn't even try? Here's why: You know that *nobody* can hold her breath for five minutes—and if you could, it would really hurt. Five seconds is a piece of cake; five minutes, and brain damage can start setting in!

Your marriage is kind of like that. Getting ready for the new baby has meant that you and your husband have had to put some romance on hold. You're "holding your breath," relationally speaking. You're not giving your marriage the oxygen we counselors call romance. That's understandable. It's hard to feel romantic when your stomach feels like it has a watermelon swimming inside it or you're constantly doing adoption paperwork (or jumping every time the phone rings, hoping it's that long-waited-for referral). And your marriage can sustain itself while you hold your breath for this short season.

But now that the watermelon is outside your body (or, if she's a chosen child, no longer just paperwork and dreams) and wearing diapers, do you still need to keep holding your breath?

"Dr. Leman," I can hear some of you saying, "you just don't understand. Nursing and taking care of this child make me tired all day long. To go out at night, I'd have to take a shower, find some clothes that are clean, iron them, put on some makeup, find a babysitter, and then try not to fall asleep at 7:00 P.M. Just the thought overwhelms me. And when we get home, he's going to want to have sex."

I'm not asking you to do something every day. I'm asking you to make a one-time commitment that will pay bigger dividends than you can ever know. When physical healing permits and you know your body can handle sexual relations again, make a big deal about it. The normal time frame given to resume sexual relations is six weeks, though this is a very arbitrary number. Physiologically, you can have sex any time the bleeding stops, which is usually complete by fourteen to twenty-one days, but that doesn't mean your body will feel ready for sexual relations, and you needn't feel obligated to rush things. Particularly if you had an episiotomy, you're going to need a little extra time to heal. But when you know you're ready, make getting started again a special event.

Admittedly, resuming sexual relations is often an afterthought for many young mothers. Six weeks can pass and they don't even miss it! They are so caught up with caring for a newborn, and their body is still adjusting from being pregnant, they wouldn't mind waiting for twelve weeks or more.

But your "other child" is probably not so eager to keep waiting and that "other child" is very important to your infant's long-term well-being. Out of concern for your

husband, I'd like to encourage you to at least consider the prospect of sexual intimacy as soon as your body will allow it.

In fact, I recommend that you make the first time particularly special. Pick your husband up after work, take him somewhere overnight, and look as enthusiastic as you can, even in the midst of your exhaustion: "It's been a long time, honey, and I can't wait to make love to you again." Make sure your husband knows how much you've missed sex too.

Because of your body's changes, do yourself a favor and bring along a lubricant, such as K-Y jelly or Astroglide. Even if you've never needed a lubricant before, your body's sudden drop in estrogen levels and a few physiological postpartum changes may reduce your natural lubrication. Having a little help will make the first time back more enjoyable for both of you.

Another big change in your romantic life, particularly if you're nursing, has to do with your breasts. They are bigger now than they have ever been, and hubby may be more interested in them than ever. But let's face it: Breasts used for nursing are fire hoses just waiting to explode! You may have to wear a nursing bra with pads to bed—and you may still leak. It can help to nurse your baby just before you begin sexual relations, but this isn't foolproof. Besides, breasts used for nursing have one thing in common (at least early on): sore, often chapped nipples. Don't expect your spouse to just "know" this. Be honest with your husband and explain what's going on. He might be disappointed, but he'll get over it.

After sex has been resumed, maybe once a month, keep doing something special to add to your regular times of sexual intimacy. Take your husband to a very private, secure place while a friend watches your kid for an hour. Remind him what "afternoon delight" means. These little forays won't take long, but your husband will be very grateful. You won't have the time or energy to do this every week, but can't you do something special once a month?

I realize that exhaustion will accompany you to bed most nights, making even the best of intentions wilt under the weight of weariness. But I hope you remember that your husband's sexual time clock will continue to tick even when yours has stopped. Even before you're ready to resume sexual intercourse, you can be very creative and loving to him and satisfy his needs without using parts of your body that are temporarily out of commission. (For more help on the subject of sex within marriage, you can read my book *Sheet Music*.) I don't want to get too explicit here, but you know what I'm talking about: Let your fingers do the walking! It'll be less stressful for you, you won't feel like you have to put on a show, and your husband will be thankful that he has such a sensitive wife.

More importantly, when you do this you're pouring much needed oxygen back into your marriage. Ultimately, the little person served most by that will be your firstborn child; she's the one who will reap the benefits of being raised in a healthy, happy marriage.

133

BACKSEAT DADS

A common complaint I hear from young mothers is that their husband shows remarkably little interest in helping out with the new baby. The mom can't understand this, because the baby has become her entire world. She can't keep herself from kissing her baby all day long, and yet here's Dad, who hasn't seen the baby all day, coming home, getting his golf clubs, and going out to hit a large bucket of balls. The wives ask me point-blank, "What's wrong with him?"

Avoid actions that scare husbands away.

A couple things are going on here that you need to know about. Many of us men took a "backseat" when it came to parenting our firstborn for a very understandable reason: Our wives were so competent that we felt we just weren't needed. The way a guy thinks is this: *Baby needs to be taken care of, but Mommy is doing a super job, so I guess that leaves me free to go do something else.* It may sound crazy to you, but that's the problem-solving mind-set of a guy. It doesn't mean he doesn't love you or the child—and it doesn't mean he doesn't want to be involved.

Another reason guys may not help out is that they get *"should*ed" away. By that I mean when they do manage to change a diaper, the wife laughs and says: "Don't you know how to put on a diaper?! You've got it on backwards!" And then the hubby hears his wife laughing about the entire episode the next time she talks to her mom or her best girl-friend.

It only takes one such occurrence for a man to decide that he's never going to change another diaper again.

Other "should" comments that scare husbands away:

- "No, honey, she likes to be burped this way."

- "Silly, her nap isn't for another hour or so."
- "Did you remember to put lotion on her bottom before you put the clean diaper on?"
- "Don't be so rough with her; she's just a baby!"

After just a few of these comments, your husband is likely to shut down. You can't make your husband get more interested in your child but you can, sadly enough, discourage him from helping. Every man wants to be a hero, but not enough women let us be heroes—they want us to do everything a certain way (i.e., their way) and are apt to ridicule us if we do anything just a little bit differently.

The marriages that transition most easily into the childrearing years are marriages in which the wife learns how to appreciate the different way that her husband cares for the baby, and in which she respects the husband's unique role in her child's life. Let's look at each of these in turn.

135
• • • • •

Secret #1: Appreciate your husband's differences.

Here's a little secret: From the male perspective, your husband is kind of thinking about the new baby as a sort of really cool toy with legs. He might not put it in just those words, but just sit back this evening and watch your husband play with the baby—as baby gets older, he'll throw her in the air and catch her. Even now he may swoop around the room with her. Though he will have his gentle moments, he'll also have his "rougher" moments. And you know what? That's how it should be.

Babies need mommies and babies need daddies. Babies don't need daddies to act like mommies or mommies who try to act like daddies. Allow your husband to be a guy around your baby. That kid is more durable than you realize, and though you probably do understand how baby likes to be burped, as long as dad can produce the desired results, does the process particularly matter?

I may even grant that your way of mothering is the best way, but I will strongly argue against you if you try to say that your way of caring is the *only* way. That's the kind of thinking that drives men crazy—and ultimately makes them shut down.

It's important that you respect these differences early on, because you want your husband to be very involved in this child's life. Every piece of research I've seen reveals that "as goes Dad, so goes the child." A father leaves an indelible imprint on his daughter (for more on this, see my book *What a Difference a Daddy Makes*). Your husband is the primary building block on which your daughter will internalize what trust is all about. He is the model by which she will measure every man who vies for her affections. If your husband is a healthy influence, odds are overwhelming that she will choose a good man to be her husband. If your husband is a negative influence, she will feel strangely drawn to dangerous men.

If your baby is a boy, your husband will become a picture of all that child wants to become himself. Your son will emulate both the good and the bad and even the quirky. I was riding in a car with my son, Kevin, when he was about three years old. Without even thinking, I cleared my throat and spit out the window. Five seconds later I heard this very tentative *pffft* and turned just in time to see Kevin attempt to spit out the same window. Unfortunately his aim was off by about twenty-four inches, so his spittle caught me mid-neck!

I just laughed about it and put it down as a father-son bonding experience. I was pretty confident that Sande would never teach Kevin how to clear his throat and spit, so I knew it was up to me.

My sister-in-law once became furious at my brother because he taught their son how to go potty outdoors. My brother likes to hunt and fish and walk in the forest, and when you're an outdoorsman, you need to learn how to answer the call of nature when you're out in the middle of the boonies with no Rest room in sight.

So far, so good, except for when my sister-in-law took my then three-year-old nephew to the mall. They walked through a courtyard area with indoor trees and plants and proceeded toward another store, when suddenly my sister-in-law realized that my nephew wasn't walking next to her anymore. She looked back in a panic and saw a small crowd gawking and shaking their heads in disgust. There was my nephew, watering one of the indoor trees, just like Daddy had taught him to do!

Now, certainly, my brother never intended to teach his son to water indoor trees in a mall. But there is something very valuable in a son or daughter's life when Dad takes the time to teach them to fish, to enjoy the outdoors, or to roughhouse in a healthy way. When dad feeds the kids, he may not make sure every food group is represented on their plate. When he takes them out to eat, he may let them get a soda and a dessert. He may eventually take your son to dinosaur movies that you think are better left unwatched. Just be thankful that your husband is involved, that he's active, that he's there. Your son or daughter needs him to be a man. Encourage your husband to parent in his own unique way, and don't "should" him out of the house.

Secret #2: Respect his role.

I'm not one to get overly strict on gender roles. As long as one of the parents stays home with the child, I'm happy. However, I also realize that in most circumstances, it's the man who goes back to work while Mommy stays home, and for good reason, especially if she has birthed this baby—she has all the equipment that Daddy lacks to care for a newborn.

If this is the case in your home, you need to respect the distant but very important role your husband is playing as provider. From your husband's perspective, meeting the family's financial needs is his main duty and focus. And now that there are three of you, he feels this drive more intensely than ever before—to take care of his family long-term. And this creates more stress on him than you might ever guess. Before you dismiss this, think about it: Your husband's financial provision is very important, assuming you want to live in a house instead of a cardboard box. Your husband might come home tired or stressed-out, but he has been working for you all day long, and that deserves some respect and appreciation. Don't judge him solely by whether he does 50 percent of the diaper changing while he's at home—unless you don't mind if he compares his paycheck to yours.

It also may surprise you—since you feel the weight of the minute-to-minute responsibility for this child—that your husband feels this weight too. You're not the only one impacted by the arrival of this child. Many men feel helpless around an infant and overwhelmingly extra-responsible for their family's welfare now that a child is involved. And men have told me they feel even more this way when they have a daughter. They think, *She's so little, so fragile. I really need to protect my little girl.* This responsibility can at times make a man feel inept—as if he's a failure. Men feel the provider role every bit as heavily as you're feeling the nurturing role.

Having said that, it's certainly reasonable for you to expect him to be an involved father. If you think your husband is getting out of balance, putting too much time and energy toward work and not enough at home, first try to understand the pressure he's feeling. Maybe he thinks he has to put in those extra hours or he'll lose his job. He wants to be there for you, but secretly he's scared his paycheck is going to fly away. In his mind it might be "first things first"—secure the paycheck, then be more present at home.

Make sure you begin the conversation by affirming his role as provider. Tell him in words he can hear how much you appreciate his hard work on your family's behalf. Then and only then have you earned the right to gently suggest that you're hoping for a little more involvement from him. You might say something like this:

"Honey, I know you've been working really hard and I really do appreciate all the hours you're putting in so we can pay the bills and live in this house. I want you to know that I pray for you every day, and the first thing I tell God is 'thank you for giving me such a hardworking husband.'

"I do wish, though, that you'd give a bit more attention to the baby. Sometimes it seems like you spend more time in front of the television than you do playing with your daughter, and that concerns me. I know you need your downtime, but the baby needs time with you too. This is really important, not just to our kid, but to me. I didn't marry you so that I could be a single parent, but a copartner. I know that dads make a big difference in their kids' lives, and you have something to give that I can't. Is there something I'm doing that's holding you back from being more involved?"

When your husband responds, really listen—and don't be defensive. If you are doing or saying something to discourage him from becoming more of an active dad, don't you want to know now—instead of years down the road? And don't try to tell him why his way is wrong. Work toward understanding, just as you did in other areas of your marriage before you had this child. This isn't about who's right and who's wrong, but about how the two of you can adjust to the new responsibilities brought about by bringing a child into your family.

THIS MIGHT SURPRISE YOU

I've been a man my entire life. Some of my best friends are men. I counsel men all the time. This has given me a certain understanding of men that I'd like to share with you (for more on this, see my book *Making Sense of the Men in Your Life*).

Men tend to get better with age. Sometimes we do better as grandfathers than we do as fathers. Some of us spend more time with the fourth child than we did with the first. It takes us time to get going. We're not the natural nurturers that mothers are. Give us time.

We want to be your hero. We may not always act like it, going out to play golf or darts or inviting a bunch of buddies to watch the big game without thinking about cleaning up the house or interrupting baby's naptime. But deep down, we really do want to be your hero. Work at bringing out the best in us. Praise what you want to see repeated. And then give us opportunities to come through for you. If we're not made to feel stupid, we'll go to the ends of the earth to be your hero.

Positive reinforcement works better with us than negative nagging. You'll get more out of a compliment than you will out of a complaint. You'll get us to be more involved with the family, for instance, by being sexually available than you will by "holding out" to punish us.

If you really want to understand us, have a baby boy, watch him grow, and realize that, in a way, even grown men are "baby boys" eager to please the main women in their lives. Early on, that's our mom. Later on, that woman is our wife. You can learn more about your husband by raising a son than you ever will from reading books or exchanging stories with your girlfriends.

8

Here Comes the Firstborn: Birth Order Bang

You can't get much more competitive than former Chicago Bears coach Mike Ditka. His 1985 Super Bowl winning team was known for its smash-mouth style of play, which mirrored the fiery personality of their coach. You might think that in retirement Coach Ditka would mellow out a bit.

Not a chance.

Now an avid golfer, Mike apparently doesn't know the meaning of the phrase "Let's take it easy." As a football player and coach, Mike saw more than his share of blood in the midst of competition. Blood and football go together. But blood and golf?

Well, when you're Mike Ditka, those words apparently *do* belong together.

One time Mike missed a short putt. Now, having played golf, I don't expect anyone to respond with a simple *tsk, tsk,* but Mike was so frustrated he decided to retire his ball by hitting it "baseball style" with his putter. He threw the little white golf ball in the air, then swung his putter like he was going to hit a grand-slam home run at Wrigley Field.

The only problem was, his playing partner happened to bend over just as Coach Ditka was going through his follow-through.

"I hit him in the forehead and took a bunch of skin off him," Mike told *Sports Illustrated*. "He was on blood thinners at the time, so it was a heck of a time getting him to stop bleeding."

But that's nothing compared to the time Mike made *himself* bleed. Once again the culprit was a missed short putt. "It was the 18th hole, and instead of acting like a human being, I took the putter and bent it behind my back," Mike recounts, "which was O.K. Trouble was, it snapped and the jagged end went in behind my ear."

Fortunately Mike was playing with a doctor, who was able to stop the bleeding, but Mike was in a hurry. Seems he had been hired to give a speech downtown. He quickly changed his clothes, then made it to the convention just in time. In the middle of his talk, Mike noticed that the crowd suddenly started looking horrified.

Finally it occurred to him what must be happening. "You know how when you start talking your adrenaline gets going and the blood flows? Well, I was wearing a powder-blue sport coat, and I look down and blood was running from behind my ear, onto my neck, over my shirt and all over my coat. I stopped and found a towel, and I said, 'If you don't mind, I'll hold a towel over this.' I finished the speech and went to the hospital and got 40 stitches."

For some people, football and golf represent fun and recreation. For others, they represent Competition with a capital *C*.

The same is true in life—some people (typically lastborns) come out of the womb laughing and having a good time. Others make their way out of their mom's bodies holding onto a clipboard to signify "I'm in charge."

That would be the firstborn.

Now, if you're a firstborn yourself, raising a firstborn,

you're going to witness Mike Ditka playing Mike Ditka—and it may get bloody! If you're a lastborn child, you may find that your firstborn baby figures out how to wrap you around his little one-half-inch finger! And if you're a middle child, you're going to experience an entirely different challenge.

THE MAIN EVENT: FIRSTBORN MEETS FIRSTBORN

When firstborn mom meets firstborn child, think "the Thrilla in Manila." Rocky Balboa against Apollo Creed. The Dallas Cowboys versus the Washington Redskins. The Boston Red Sox against the New York Yankees.

In other words, it's "the main event"—competition at its fiercest!

The child that is of your own birth order is, in all probability, the child you're most likely to bang heads with. And since firstborns like to be in charge—and only one person *can* be in charge—firstborn on firstborn tends to be the most toxic mix.

Our family is no different. I'm the fun-loving lastborn, and I had the good sense to marry a firstborn. Sande is more than a firstborn—she's also a stubborn German. When Holly, our first child, came into the world, you would have thought somebody had thrown a Redskin and Cowboy fan into the same room. The sparks flew!

Even today I notice the occasional tension. Holly and Sande are in business together, and both of them excel at pointing fingers at each other.

Don't get me wrong: they have a wonderful and close mother/daughter relationship. But as two firstborns, there will always be a bit of "iron striking iron" between them.

I remember when Holly was just a baby. Sande came into

145
* * * * *

the living room and said, "Honey, would you wake up Holly? We need to leave."

"*I'm* not waking her up," I said. "I woke her up yesterday. It's *your* turn to wake her up."

Sande sighed in resignation and turned.

"You want to borrow my old football helmet?" I asked her.

You see, Holly woke up swinging if her naps were cut off by more than thirty seconds. You've heard of the "divine right of kings"? Well, firstborns think they have the divine right of schedule. The entire family is supposed to bend around their personality. We called Holly "Judge Judy" long before she got a job as vice-principal of a school—which suits her perfectly. I can't imagine a better person to have in charge of a school than our Holly.

Keep in mind, you don't really have to be the oldest in your family to have a firstborn personality. For instance, if you're the only daughter in a family of boys, or if there's a gap of five years or more between you and the next oldest child, or if the child above you had physical or developmental challenges, you may have "skipped" orders and become a *de facto* firstborn.

You know something else that creates a firstborn personality? A critical parent. You have to guard against this natural bent if your birth order pushes you in that direction—especially when you're a firstborn mom bringing home a firstborn child. By your standing as a firstborn, you could probably make a living espousing flaws (beginning with yourself, of course). In certain situations, that's a marketable skill: When you need a quality-control officer at a factory, for instance, by all means, hire a firstborn! But the skill that would help you excel at meticulously hanging wallpaper, being an accountant, or taking on the responsibilities of a CEO, will get you in trouble with your kid or your husband.

Let me put it this way: If you're the spouse or child of a flaw picker, it gets real old, real quick.

So, firstborn mom, let me give you a little Lemanly advice: Dial it back a bit. Your baby's development may not follow the ten guidebooks you've read. In the end it doesn't matter whether she crawls at six months or nine months; nor will your mothering abilities be judged on whether she gets out of diapers by her second birthday. It won't make a centimeter's worth of difference by the time she graduates from high school as to how soon she achieved this or that physical achievement. But it will matter tremendously—more than you can imagine, in fact—that she had a warm, loving, and accepting mom. This baby craves your acceptance. If you keep it in the front of your mind that your bent will be to expect too much from this kid, you'll be able to catch yourself and work at encouraging rather than constantly correcting.

In fact, put a bookmark on this page and regularly ask yourself these questions. I've written them based on the firstborn's natural bent:

1. Am I getting myself and my child involved in too many activities? Am I worried about scheduling playtime, music time, recreational time, art time, etc., with the result that I scarcely have time to think or rest myself? Remember, Mom, if you're tired, you're not going to be at your best—and you'll probably take it out on your baby, because that's who you're with most of the time.

2. Am I trying to be the perfect mom, or am I focusing on being an excellent mom? Am I asking too much of myself? Parenting is a twenty-four-hour a day, eighteen-year job—nobody hits grand slams every time they get up to bat. Give yourself a break; you're

going to have good days and bad days. If you harp on yourself because you had one bad day, or one frustrated outburst, you'll drive yourself crazy with guilt.

3. Am I a slave to my to-do list? Do I act like it's a crime if I have to let laundry go, or allow a room to get messy? It's okay to occasionally leave a few dirty dishes in the sink while you tend to more important matters.

4. Am I obsessed with how others think of me? Do I put too much time and effort into what kinds of clothes my kids are wearing so that everyone will think I'm the perfect mom?

5. Do I criticize my husband for doing things differently? Does he have a hard time pleasing me, because he doesn't clean the bottle thoroughly enough, or put the diaper on the right way, or choose the right matching clothes for baby to wear? Listen, Mom, you want your husband to be a useful ally. Don't turn him into an enemy by making him feel stupid or incompetent. You'll need all the help you can get.

PARENTING THE FIRSTBORN

If you're not a firstborn, you may not understand the firstborn's natural bent toward perfectionism, so you may not be as sensitive to how much damage you can do by "shoulding" your kid all the time. Stressing the "shoulds" reinforces your firstborn's tendency to already be critical toward himself. Every "should" is like waving a red flag in front of a bull: "You should be doing this! You should be doing that! Why can't you get this right? How many times do I have to tell you that the blocks go on the *lower* shelf and the puzzles go on the *upper shelf?*"

Look, Mom, if junior is putting the toys away, he's done his job. Just because you're hypersensitive about everything being in order doesn't mean a two- to four-year-old needs to be!

As we talked about before, learn to accept a few wrinkles on the bedspread, or a few mispronounced words. The world won't stop spinning on its axis if you let a few mispro-nounced words go by and instead learn to enjoy your child's learning curve. I don't golf much anymore, but when I used to, I couldn't stand to hear some fathers deconstruct every tiny flaw in their boy's golf swing: "Your hands are too far behind the ball. Keep more balanced in your stance. Don't hold the club so tightly. Keep your head still." I was sick of hearing the constant instruction, and it wasn't even directed at me!

149

Nit-picking conveys that your child has fallen short and isn't measuring up. Keep that up, and I guarantee you they'll find their way into my office in another two decades. Too many firstborns already see their value based on what they do as opposed to who they are, and they pay counselors like me good money to break out of this harmful mold! Wouldn't you rather they save that money and spend it on your grandchil-dren instead of sitting in some shrink's office to talk about *you*?

Since firstborns naturally develop their own rules (God have mercy on you if you try to break the normal bedtime routine, for instance, or put the bear where the stuffed giraffe usually goes), be careful about stacking on more rules. Since you want to help this child become more relational in spite of herself, try to get her to think socially instead of by rules. Your mantra should be: *People matter more than proce-dure*. The fact that your child feels loved and accepted is far more important than that the puzzles and blocks end up on the "right" shelf.

With your firstborn, you'll have to be very particular about the specific rules you do have. Remember in an earlier chapter when I talked about how Holly wouldn't accept it when I said "We'll leave *around* nine o'clock?" Firstborns need the exact time, and the exact order: First you brush your teeth, then you wash your face, then you get dressed, then put on your socks and shoes, and then you can go outside to play. This isn't meant to contradict what I said earlier about not laying on more rules; it means that you accept the fact that firstborns like specific procedure, so you take the time to lay things out from A to Z. If they break the routine, it's no big deal; the routine is there to help them process what needs to be done, not to hold them prisoner.

Because of a few quirks surrounding her birth, our little Lauren actually has a firstborn personality. Lauren doesn't admit this: she likes to remind me that she's the baby, but then I tell her how, at two-and-a-half years of age, she lined up her cassettes in perfect order. If you moved so much as one of those cassettes from its proper place, you heard about it! And when we took our Yamaha Wave Runner jet ski out on the lake, with the digitized speedometer, Lauren would scream bloody murder if you went over 4. She didn't want you to go 3 or 5 or 4.5—you had to keep that sucker on 4.

When child number two (or three or four) comes along, remember that the firstborn should receive special privileges along with additional responsibilities. The firstborn will always want to feel special, and that's okay, provided that he realizes being "special" (i.e., staying up later, reading books not appropriate for younger readers) also means doing extra work that younger hands aren't up to.

Also, give your firstborn some "two on one" time—two parents, one kid. Firstborns tend to gravitate toward adults. They practically see themselves as adults, to be honest with you, and they enjoy the conversation they can have with both their parents. Respect this need. It's a helpful counterbalance to the fact of life that, during the day, Mom will probably have to spend more time with the younger children than she can with the firstborn, since the firstborn can fend for himself much better than the others can.

Finally, *relax*. Children pick up on our own tension, and this is doubly true of firstborns. I want you to *enjoy* this time. You'll never get to raise a firstborn again! This is it—your one chance! As I'm writing this, Krissy, my secondborn, is expecting our first grandchild. She and her husband were with us at a restaurant, and when they saw the waitress pull out a high-chair that looked less than new, Krissy commented to her husband, "When Conner (they already have him named) gets here, we're going to bring our *own* high-chair to restaurants."

As gently as I could, I said, "Krissy, a little dirt won't kill your child." If you only knew what your kid was eating behind your back (paste, pencils, dog food, and worse), you'd cringe! Having them sit at a high-chair that isn't thrown out and replaced every time it's used is not that big a deal.

To all firstborn moms, I want to say, keep the big picture in mind. Don't major in the minors. Every child will spill things on occasion. That doesn't mean he's on his way to becoming a serial murderer. And don't set up battles you can't win: "Listen, young lady, you will eat your peas, or you'll sit there for the rest of your life!" Your firstborn may just take you up on that.

I'm not saying you should let everything slide: You should have zero toleration for a two-year-old who sasses you or hits you, for instance, but please, let the little things slide.

LOVING LIFE AS A LASTBORN

I was asked to be the keynote speaker at a conference being attended by my older sister Sally, a firstborn to the core. It was nine o'clock, and we were eating breakfast; my session began at ten.

Over our eggs and potatoes, Sally asked me, "So what are you speaking on this morning?"

I shrugged. "Don't know. I haven't decided yet."

"What do you mean you haven't decided yet? You're going to be standing on that stage in front of thousands of people in less than an hour!"

"I know. But I want to look at them first before I decide what to speak on."

Sally lost her appetite. "You're making my stomach churn just listening to you; I'm more nervous than you can believe just hearing you say that."

You see, firstborn Sally would have had the speech written out weeks before the conference and probably would have delivered it to the mirror at least a dozen times. But my best talks always come when I'm not using any notes, when I simply try to read the crowd, connect with them, and shape my words accordingly.

Welcome to the world of the lastborn parent. If you're a lastborn personality, you probably love spontaneity as much as the firstborn hates it. You like to be the life of the party, the center of attention, and you can't stand rules (although you *love* breaking them). We're the practical jokers fighting against the legacy set by our rule-following, high-achieving, older siblings. On the positive side, we're great people persons. We can live with ambivalence. We're not afraid to take risks, and we can be as persistent as a junkyard dog going after a bone. We also tend to be a lot of fun to be around.

But when we have to raise a firstborn, things can get a little dicey. First off, we're not likely to put too many rules on our kids. We never liked rules, and we don't like to lay down rules either. That's good. But sometimes we lastborns can be a little *too* unstructured.

I remember when Sande left me alone with one of our children. I could tell she was nervous about being gone overnight, but I assured her I was more than up to the task. She had absolutely nothing to worry about.

Later that night Sande called to see how things were going. Eager to impress my wife with my parenting skills, I talked about the fun Lauren and I had, the things we did, the crafts we made, the places we visited—all things that I'm sure this kid never got to do with Sande.

153

"What has she eaten?" Sande asked.

"Eaten?" I asked.

Doggone it, I knew I had forgotten something! I never fed the little critter! We had been having such a good time, I forgot she needed to eat!

If you're a firstborn, you can't imagine how that could happen. If you're a lastborn, you probably have your own stories to tell. We lastborns hate to let little rules—like eating three times a day—get in the way of our good times.

Listen up, all you lastborns: Babies need structure, and firstborn babies in particular. We can't hide behind our birth order on this one. We're going to have to grow up a bit to be a good parent. It may not be necessary for us to set the egg timer to know when we need to change the diaper (as a firstborn is likely to do), nor do we have to worry about having breakfast at eight, lunch at noon, and dinner at five every day, without fail, plus or minus three minutes. But we do have to feed them, and we should make sure they don't walk around with a wet, full diaper that weighs more than they do.

You're taking on a big responsibility. No longer can you be the center of attention: You must focus on your child. That's hard for us lastborns to do!

Also, you're going to have to learn to pick up a bit. We tend to be rather messy, but if you're not careful, your entire floor will be covered in dirty clothes and diapers. It's amazing how quickly a child can fill the laundry basket. If we're *too* messy, we might create a situation that simply isn't healthy for a baby. Especially when your child starts crawling around, you've got to focus on not being so absentminded. Never leave anything within arm's reach that you don't want to go in your baby's mouth.

Also—and this is going to be hard for you—you're going to have to get used to living on a schedule. Firstborn babies thrive in orderly environments. They do best when they eat, sleep, and are bathed according to a regular routine. When all this is done in a haphazard manner, to a baby it feels like chaos. Babies don't like chaos. Babies tend to cry when they face chaos. Crying babies make moms get even more frazzled, interrupting the schedule even more, which creates even more chaos, which makes the baby cry more, and—you get the picture.

MYSTERIOUS MIDDLES

Okay, all you middle moms, don't feel left out—even though I know you will. You got squeezed out of the photo album, between Super Sam, the firstborn, and Cute Courtney, the lastborn, with the result that you have the fewest pictures in the family photo album. Guess what? You're also going to have the shortest section in this book, and there's a reason for that: You probably already have just about the right disposition to raise a firstborn. You're less intense than most firstborns, but a tad bit more responsible than the lastborns. In short, you don't really need special advice.

Middleborns tend to be the most mysterious birth order blend because they often play off of the child born in front of them: If the firstborn is an athlete, the secondborn often becomes a science geek, or vice versa. It's much harder to peg a middle, because different middles go in different directions. For instance, some middles are quiet and shy; others are very sociable and outgoing. Some are laid back; others are impatient and easily frustrated. Some middles are very competitive, eager to topple their older siblings; others are easygoing. While a few play the role of rebel, most are usually pretty good mediators.

155

• • • • •

Since middles usually have to go outside the family to obtain rewards and recognition (because they can't compete with their older siblings), they often leave home at the youngest age. But that's partly due to the fact that middles usually make more friends than firstborns and so feel more comfortable in the outside world.

Middles tend to be the most mysterious—and closed—of all the birth orders, and they are likely to be mentally tough and very independent. While they embarrass easily, they also tend to be the most loyal.

So, put a person like that in a mothering situation, and what do you get? Middle moms have a special gift that they can put into full effect: mediation. If your husband is a firstborn, be prepared to "referee" the upcoming battles between father and child (as well as between child number one and child number two). You've already been warned that the child nearest to your own birth order is usually the one most difficult to get along with, so be aware of your husband's own tendencies to butt heads with his birth order, and expect to be called on to help win back some peace and quiet.

You may have to guard against "peace at any price." Middles like compromise, but sometimes parenting is about making an absolute judgment call. You might have to work at building up enough courage to disappoint your child.

Another potential weakness is that you are probably the most reluctant birth order to seek outside help. By virtue of your birth order, you've learned to go it alone and make it on your own. Thus when you get tired, you're less likely to call Grandma or even your husband and admit that you just need a break. Do yourself a favor here: occasionally act like a lastborn, who wouldn't even hesitate to impose on somebody else!

A SECOND CHANCE

Regardless of your birth order, raising this child will do more for you than you may ever realize. One of the fun things that can happen is that you may begin to understand yourself a little better. Having been duly warned about your own birth order's strengths and weaknesses, I'd like to encourage you to use that knowledge to help you better relate to others.

We don't get many second chances in this life—but this is one. You're starting a brand-new family. You're creating entirely new traditions. You're laying the groundwork for memories that your children will carry to their graves—and likely affect how they raise their own children as well.

Your baby will learn what life is like through you. Her worldview will be largely determined by the world you present. Do you want to present a world that's loving, comforting, warm, and close? Or that's critical, threatening, insecure, and abusive?

I know you want to give your child the best start possible.

To do that, you'll have to use the information we've shared to challenge yourself as you parent your child. It's a rare opportunity to work on your own maturity.

Take full advantage of this second chance!

9

Toddler Time

Now that your baby is one year old, let's talk about college.

"Wait a minute, Dr. Leman," I can hear some of you saying. "Don't you think that's rushing things a bit?"

Not at all!

I don't care which college your son or daughter goes to, or even if your son or daughter goes to college. But I want you to think of college age as the time when the fruits of your parenting labor will be either bitter or sweet.

Put it this way: When you take this tyke, who is now sleeping peacefully in his crib, and drop this child—at seventeen or eighteen years of age—at the college dorm, what would you like this child to be like? Do you want a giving son or a taking son? Do you want a daughter who is thoughtful of others or who is self-centered? Do you want a son who is powerless to stare down his peer group or a strong young man whom others follow?

I hope you want your child to be responsible, to care about others, to share your moral values, and to have a strong faith in God. If he is all this, you won't be so concerned with whether he becomes a police officer, a meteorologist, or a congressman—you'll be proud of his character and eager to let everybody know that this fine young man is your son.

THE KEY TO DASHED—OR FULFILLED—DREAMS

Every mother probably has similar visions for her child—after all, what mother wouldn't want these qualities in her child? But, sadly, many of these dreams are dashed even before the child reaches adolescence. Why is this?

The answer is in the early years of your child's life. Most often, the culprit is poor discipline. If you love your child, you will discipline him—not over- or underdiscipline him, but discipline him just right (as we talked about earlier in this book). And that's why I'm dedicating this entire chapter to that important subject.

Please let me reiterate here that I don't equate discipline with spanking. Particularly for an infant, spanking is inappropriate. Later on (after the age of two), discipline may involve an occasional swat on the bum, but for now, the best way to discipline your young child is to live a disciplined life.

So get your child on an eating and sleeping schedule (see chapter 3) that you carefully maintain. Work out doable bedtime schedules, and stick to them. Children feel most comfortable with a set routine. Be a parent of integrity: let your "no" mean *no* and not *No, unless you keep whining for another hour, in which case I'll give in just so you shut up.* Discipline is not really something you pass down to your child or even do to your child, as much as it is the life you live as an adult in front of your child.

PUT THE LONG-TERM FIRST

Some of you have already decided not to discipline your child, in part by ignoring my earlier advice to get out of the house, alone as a couple, within the first two weeks. (See, I caught you!) You read that suggestion and thought, *Oh, Dr.*

Leman, you don't understand. I could never leave my baby for two hours. I love her too much for that. You must have written that for other moms, but not for me.

Excuse me, but if you really did love your baby that much, you'd put her long-term good ahead of your own insecurities and continue to keep the romance alive in your marriage! Going out and leaving baby alone is where discipline starts, because right away you're telling your child by your actions, *You are very important to us, but we will not cater to your every whim. You are dependent on us and we will work hard to meet your needs, but the world does not revolve solely around you.*

Our goal as parents isn't to create a pseudo-utopian state where the child is happy at every moment. (Remember what I said earlier about an "unhappy" child being a "healthy" child? Children need to discover, early on, that not everything in life will be perfect or go their way.) Home is a place where kids learn to fail in a warm, friendly environment; where they understand that sometimes they have to sacrifice for the common good; and where they experience the joy of contributing to a group effort.

161
• • • • •

If you've gotten off to a shaky start, don't freak out. Just go back over the early chapters of this book and put those suggestions into practice. They are not arbitrary routines that are designed simply to keep your child healthy and alive. On the contrary, I suggest them because they have the power to shape your child's very soul.

BEWARE CHANGING RITUALS OR ROUTINES!

When kids live in chaos—wondering when dinner is going to be served, taking naps at a different time every day, not understanding how nighttime bed is different from a daytime nap because no ritual has been established—they grow frustrated and angry because everything always seems new and confusing. Rituals and discipline provide security, understanding, and ultimately, happier kids. This will set a pattern for the rest of your child's life—and even carry on, incredibly, to the next generation.

Does this really work? The Leman household is living proof. No, we're not perfect, but we have done many things right with our five kids. For instance, the Lemans have never had arguments about whether our children could be involved in different activities five nights a week because our children learned early on that dinnertime is family time. We don't make exceptions lightly. We will allow visitors to come to our dinner table, but we won't glibly allow our kids to become visitors at other tables if we feel the family has been getting too little attention.

Such routines and rituals provide security and a sense of belonging. Kids thrive in such an environment. You'll be amazed at how quickly they catch on to various routines, and how important those routines are even when they don't understand them. When Mom rocks baby in a special chair, reads him a story, and then says a prayer, he knows that he is going to be in bed all night; this isn't just a nap. And his body clock has learned to adjust, expecting breakfast, lunch, and dinner at a particular time. If these times are respected, baby won't complain, because that's how things are supposed to be.

If you don't believe me, try this experiment: Establish a routine with your child for at least fourteen days, and then try to break it. You'll see soon enough how important these routines are to most children—of any age!

Sande and I learned this lesson the hard way. Just before the first printing of *Making Children Mind without Losing Yours*, I got a phone call from my publisher, telling me they needed a picture of our family—tomorrow. It was Sunday afternoon and the only place still open was Sears. Holly was taking a nap, so we did what I've already told you not to do: We broke her routine and woke her up.

Mind you, we did this with fear and trepidation. The worst job in the world, below cleaning out outhouses and tarring a Texas roof in August, had to be waking up Holly from a nap. From the time she was a baby, Sande and I had many an argument about whose turn it was to tap the tiny tyrant on the shoulder and get her out of bed.

Waking up a child prematurely reminds me of passing those warning signs posted along the Niagara River, near to where I spend the summers. If you wade out past these warning signs, you're liable to get sucked into the current and pulled down the falls, suddenly unable to stop or turn around. It's the dreaded "point of no return."

163

This "point of no return" is a good lesson for young parents to learn, because sometimes you see the same thing with kids: You recognize that you've crossed the point where they're coming undone, and things will only get worse unless you just walk away. Once kids tumble down this slippery slope, there's no climbing back up.

But due to my obligations to my publisher, we couldn't just walk away. That Sunday afternoon we had to have a family picture taken.

We finally got Holly up, but it was nearly impossible to get her dressed. Nothing fit right.

"This label itches. . . . The sleeves are too tight. . . . This dress is too long. . . . This dress is too short. . . . These socks feel funny. . . . These shoes feel like they're going to fall off."

I had had enough, made her stay in what she was already wearing, and took her, literally screaming and kicking, out of her room.

Then we made mistake number two. Because Holly had

fallen asleep, she hadn't eaten lunch. Due to the fact that it had taken so long to get Holly dressed, we were in near panic mode and didn't want to pause to get her something to eat. We were running seriously late, after all, and you could feel the pressure rising. Don't for a second think your kids don't notice when you're uptight. They live for moments such as these: *Oh, Mommy and Daddy are trying to give me the rush job, are they? Well, I'll show them. I'm feeling a little bit slow today.*

We handed Holly a banana, which she promptly proceeded to smash into Sande's face. Attila the Hun meets Judge Judy—that was our firstborn!

Sande went to repair her makeup while I took our screaming firstborn to the car, all so that we could have a nice family portrait for my latest childrearing book. I fastened Holly in her car seat, wondering what the publishers would say when one of the people in the photo had red puffy eyes and the mom had banana smeared all over her face.

Once we got to Sears, we tried to splash water on Holly's face to take care of the red puffy eyes, but this just irritated her more. It took longer than you could believe for the photographer to get even one remotely acceptable picture. It wasn't a prize-winning photograph by any means, but it was better than anything else we could have gotten that day.

I know better now. If a publisher were to call me with a similar request today, I'd be far more forceful: "I can't do it. We'll get it taken tomorrow and overnight it so that you'll have it by Tuesday, but I'm not going to get it done today."

THE ALPHA DOG

Another very important disciplinary effect of routines is that they help cut off some of those troublesome power struggles. And with firstborns in particular, power struggles can quickly become a way of life. At a very young age, kids begin building agendas and think they know how life ought to be. Routines that you establish help reinforce the truth that you are not a servant to the child—you're a mom to the child. And there's a big difference between the two.

But since power struggles are so often a part of the first-born parenting experience, let's spend some more time talking about them.

When she was just nine years old, our youngest daughter, Lauren, got a new cocker spaniel puppy named Rosie. I told Lauren that she was going to be this puppy's mommy. I wanted her to think like that, knowing that raising a puppy can provide many valuable lessons as Lauren approaches adolescence.

165
• • • • •

As anybody who has trained puppies knows, dogs are ultimately descended from wolves. They have a pack mentality, and the law of the pack is this: "Friends" can be ignored, disagreed with, or even fought with, but the Alpha dog must always be obeyed.

If you watch a little puppy bother its mother and you hear the mother growl, you're going to see that puppy drop its head onto the floor in a sign of submission. Basically, that puppy is saying, "You win." If another puppy growls, the first puppy will growl or bite back—but the puppy will never question the Alpha dog.

Lauren had to learn that if she just wanted to be friends with Rosie, life wouldn't be much fun. Until Rosie sees Lauren as the Alpha dog, she'll feel free to obey or disobey any command, depending on how she feels about that command. When Lauren takes Rosie for a walk, Rosie will either make Lauren miserable, or she'll willingly obey. If she recognizes Lauren as the Alpha dog, she'll walk by her side. If she sees Lauren as a playmate, she'll pull on that rope, cross the street at will, or stop whenever she feels like it.

As Lauren and I went over all this, it struck me how similar training a puppy is to raising a kid. Too often I talk to moms who want to be "best friends" with their children. Children need friends, but they need parents even more. If you become your child's friend, the two of you can't help but disagree. And how will you solve your disagreement? Two equals can't pull rank. The friend-to-friend approach to parenting leads to confusion and chaos. Besides, how many six-year-olds really need a twenty-seven-year-old for a "best friend"? Don't you think they'd like a best friend who actually enjoys watching *Barney* with them?

Like just about every puppy, Rosie had her moments of "nipping." Good breeds won't actually attack a person, but they'll put your fingers or arm in their mouth and playfully let you know they have teeth. This is something a good pet owner won't allow; a dog should never think he has the right to put human flesh in his mouth.

Trainers know how to handle this. One trick is to immediately put your fingers in the puppy's mouth and press downward on the back of her tongue until she whimpers while you say, "No biting!" Although this can be a very effective form of training, young kids often shy away from it for two reasons. First, they're scared. You're trying to teach your dog not to bite by deliberately putting your hand in your dog's mouth, and that takes a lot of trust—those teeth might, indeed, scrape your fingers.

Second, doing this "tongue press" usually makes the dog whimper. The kid thinks he's hurting his dog, not realizing that the whimper is exactly what you want: It's an acknowledgement of submission.

I saw a young boy work this to perfection. After days of training, he saw his dog start to nip another kid. He barked, "Out!" at his dog (a universal signal of "Stop!") and that puppy flipped over on her back and looked up at him as if to say, "I give up. What do you want me to do now?"

Sometimes I meet moms who are rendered immobile by toddler "whimpers." Just the other day, as I was walking at the mall, I saw a mother trying to pry her son off a kiddie ride. Instead of exerting her authority, this mother resorted to bribery: "Honey," she said, "now we get to go to Target to look at toys!"

What struck me was the very evident fear she had over her boy's potential displeasure. She knew he didn't want to leave the ride, and she was too terrified of him to simply say, "Son, we need to go now." So she resorted to promising something that she hoped would be even more fun— looking at toys—to get him to move. Now, how will she get him out of Target's toy section? I bet you she had to buy him a toy!

167

Are you afraid of your child's whimpers? Do you let your child rule over you because she knows that one big tantrum is the only thing she needs to do to get what she really wants? Don't be like a poor puppy trainer; recognize that good training produces a good whimper of submission now and then.

I know you didn't bring home a puppy—but you did bring home a very strong-willed child. How do I know that? Because virtually every child has a strong will! Sure, some are more strong-willed than others, but all in all, kids will drive your life if you let them. And they'll never stop.

A friend of mine had a young son who played in a golf tournament. My friend watched as one of his son's opponents teed off with a $450 driver. Every time this privileged boy made a bad shot, he hit the ground with that expensive driver.

"One more time, and you're through!" his mom warned on the first hole.

The next time the boy threw a tantrum, the mom repeated her warning: "One more time, and you're done. I'm pulling you!"

The boy got no fewer than five "one more times." On the last "one more time," the dad actually said, "That's it! You're done!" but the boy kept playing, and the parents let him.

The boy's dad explained to my friend that the expensive driver he was playing with was borrowed. He made a big deal about how the boy would have to "earn" the club by making the honor roll a certain number of times.

The tantrum-throwing boy actually did pretty well in the tournament, even though the other players and parents were appalled by the way this boy had acted. His parents rewarded his behavior by buying him the club that he had already been told he would have to earn. So you tell me— who was *really* Alpha dog in that family? And would you want that person married to your daughter, some years down the road?

You see, it won't stop at eighteen months, five years, ten years, or even eighteen years. If you allow this child to run over you now, if you tolerate abusive behavior as a toddler, your child will run your life for the rest of your life. He'll laugh at your threats because he knows you won't follow through. He'll scoff at your promised rewards because he knows that he'll be able to get what he wants without having to work for it. He knows it, because he knows he's in charge.

Your baby needs to learn sooner, rather than later, that you are the Alpha dog. Children must learn to obey you not because they agree with you or because you are able to give them five reasons why you're right. They need to listen because you're in charge.

The most important lesson I give young moms is this: "Remember: You're the mommy. You can't let this child dictate your life, and she will if you let her. Your job is not to meet her every need. I want you to immediately establish a healthy authority, and the sooner, the better."

I saw a T-shirt on a woman that said something I really like: "Because I'm the mommy, that's why."

The sooner you establish this healthy authority, the sooner you'll actually enjoy life with your baby and toddler. True democracies—where everything is decided by popular vote—can get pretty chaotic, especially in a family. You're not running a democracy at home. You're the benevolent dictator, and the sooner that is understood and accepted, the happier you and your child will be. Yes, some children will fight for control, but it's easier to deny this to a baby and a toddler than it is to try to "start over" with a teenager who is bigger and stronger than you are!

This need to teach kids to respect authority is why I urge first-time moms not to get overly concerned about dirt and messes that don't matter. You're going to have to learn where to pick your battles and what to focus on, and a healthy attitude toward authority needs to be near the top of the list. Obeying you and respecting your role as mom must never become one of ten *additional* issues that you and your child are fighting about. It must be understood, accepted, and practiced on a daily basis. It is the first battle—and if you win it, you will cut off many subsequent battles.

169

SAVE YOUR ENERGY FOR TRUE CHALLENGES

Particularly with a firstborn, there are going to be lots of things that your child is concerned about but that aren't worth fighting over. You'll be surprised at how many clothes bug firstborns; they have to wear certain colors, collars, or fabrics. If a sleeve is too long, or too short, the shirt is "ruined." When they eat, they'll develop all kinds of finicky rules, like not letting the pancake syrup actually touch the pancake, or they'll cry at the "crisis" that erupts when their spaghetti sauce accidentally touches their bread. When we took our firstborn Holly to the beach for the first time, we discovered to our dismay that Holly hated to have sand touching her hands and feet. I wiped her off, but she kept pointing at her hands and grunting until I discovered the two little grains of sand that were bugging her!

Save your energy for true challenges. If your kid doesn't want mushy pancakes, let her pour her own syrup or put the syrup on a different plate. If the kid thinks one shirt is itchy, let him pick out his own. You don't want arguing to become a way of life with a firstborn—they'll tire you out!

FROM MEETING TO LEADING

In the first three months of your baby's life, you spent the bulk of your time meeting your baby's basic needs: holding her, burping her, rocking her, feeding her, playing with her, and then putting her down for her nap.

But in a mere matter of months, your focus must shift from meeting needs to leading her into a healthy independence. I'm sure you've noticed that with every passing month this child has become more and more of an individual person. It wasn't long before the newborn could distinguish the difference between Mommy's arms, Grandma's arms, and a stranger's arms, and when she wanted to be fed, she wanted Mommy's arms!

You laughed, took your baby into your arms, and maybe even secretly were quite pleased that baby loves you best. But if you stay at this place of simply meeting your child's needs, you're setting yourself up for some major trials down the road.

You now have the opportunity, privilege, and obligation to help your child mature into her own individuality. The difficulty is that in the midst of this process, it can be very confusing trying to distinguish challenges to your authority with personality quirks. These moments can be so subtle that first-time mothers often don't recognize them for what they are. If a kid thinks whimpering, whining, rebelling, or looking frightened will break you, that's what he'll use, and since you haven't been through this, you may not realize what's going on—he's not fighting about mushy pancakes, he's fighting about control.

171
• • • • •

As a mom, your job is to understand your child's insecurities and help him deal with them in a healthy, submissive way. Let's take one common issue as an example. Imagine you're dropping your child off at preschool. I know that's still a year or two away, but it'll be here before you know it. On the first day of class you and your three-year-old are running a little late. When you arrive, most of the other kids are already settled in, coloring their name tags. You and junior walk up to the door of the room, and your son already feels like an outsider, so what does he do? He grabs your leg as if he were standing on the precipice of Mount Everest and would surely fall to his death if he let go.

You're new at this; you've never dropped off a child for the first time at preschool before, so you're not completely sure what you should do. Fortunately, Ms. Jenkins, the

teacher, has a master's degree in education and child development and says to herself, *Uh oh, I better help the stray lamb
get into the flock,* so she excuses herself, walks over to you
and your boy, drops to her knees, gets on eye level with the
kid, and gently says, "Hello, Alexander."

Alexander's first official act is to bury his head between
your legs, trying to pretend that none of this is happening.
You haven't seen him act like this in some time; it seems
like he's reverting a bit, so now you're really confused.
You wonder if you're doing the right thing in bringing him to
preschool. Should you just have waited until kindergarten?

What's going on here? Well, try to see it from his eyes:
Alexander *is* a little scared. He's never faced this situation
before. It's normal for him to act frightened. Especially if he's
never even met the teacher before or been out of your sight
for more than a few minutes.

After a little coaxing and much prying, you and Ms.
Jenkins finally get Alexander to get his head out of your body
and say a muffled "Hi." With even greater effort, Ms.
Jenkins manages to pry Alexander from your leg and escort
him over to the group.

"Everybody listen up!" she says. "I want to introduce all
of you to Alexander. Can you say 'hi' to Alexander?"

"Hiiiii Alexander," the class says in unison.

You hang around just long enough to see Alexander
happily jump into the group game. He gives you a little wave
to let you know he's okay, and you go back to your car and
cry like a baby because your firstborn is growing up and
doesn't need you anymore!

Given this scenario, what do you think will happen on
Tuesday? Will Alexander walk into the preschool like he
owns the place, give everybody high fives, and yell out,
"Well, Teach, what do you got for us today?"

172

Not likely. That's a few years down the road.

More likely, Alexander is going to hang back once again, and once again grab onto your leg like a vice. You, the first-time mom, are understandably confused. "But Alexander, remember how much fun you had yesterday?"

"No."

"Don't you want to stay again?"

"No."

Deep down Alexander probably does want to stay, but he also wants the same secure welcome he got yesterday. That introduction made the day go so well that he has decided to hold back, expecting Ms. Jenkins to come up to him once again and give him another personal escort, followed by another grand introduction. And if everybody in the class would like to say, "Hiiiii Alexander" once again, well, that would be the cherry on top of his sundae.

173

I want you, as an adult, to try to be that three-year-old just for a minute. Would you rather walk into a group situation stone cold—or wait for the sweet-smelling escort who has soft hands and an encouraging voice? I know plenty of forty-year-olds who dread mixing it up at parties, so let's not be too hard on the three-year-old.

But that doesn't mean we give in to their demands. Kids figure out pretty early how they can control situations—by being loud, obnoxious, shy, or by acting ill. I've seen it all. As long as their behavior gets them what they want, they don't really care what method you require. And they're smart enough to figure out how to get to you.

SO WHAT SHOULD YOU DO?

On the second day, stoop down to Alexander's eye level and give him a reassuring hug. "Honey, these are the same kids that were here yesterday, and look over there—there's Ms. Jenkins. You need to go to school now, that's your job, and Mommy needs to go to her job." Give him a hug and a kiss, and if he starts complaining, catch Ms. Jenkins' eye. Try to communicate, *I'm leaving, good luck,* and then go. And don't look back.

If you stand there and debate Alexander, or walk out and then hang around or come back inside the room, you're inviting him to pull out the big guns: a *grand-mal*-type temper tantrum.

On day number three, your drop-off should go even more quickly. The lesson here is one I've already stated earlier: Don't start habits that you don't want to see continued. If you don't want to debate Alexander about the merits of preschool every morning, don't get into even one debate. Once you have done something one time, your firstborn will see it as a license and privilege to keep doing it for the rest of eternity. Once you give a child a second snack at night, you have just built in the expectation that every night she can expect to get two snacks. She knows she may have to work for that second snack, but since she broke you once, she figures she can break you twice.

So on that third day, you want a clean break with Alexander. If you talk to any veteran parent, they'll tell you that while your kid might be fussing when you leave, he or she usually settles down right away. Why? There's no audience. That experienced teacher won't be played like a violin. Your kid picks up on this and puts his instrument back in his case.

Even after this third day, stay on your guard. One thing I noticed with Rosie, Lauren's dog: She was doing so well in training but then had a bad couple of days. She reverted, testing us and Lauren again to see if we really were the Alpha dogs of the family.

Your son or daughter will do this as well. Once they know their place, they'll settle down into it rather comfortably—for a while. But if they ever see your defenses weaken, they'll come out once again, guns blazing, challenging your authority. You must consistently stay in charge. Your child needs you to maintain your authority.

IN A NUTSHELL

This may sound a bit repetitive, but this parenting issue is so important I want to make sure you're getting it. Here is what we've talked about in "nutshell" form.

How do you discipline a toddler (or an infant, for that matter)? You discipline a toddler by living a disciplined life. You do things that are good for you and good for your marriage. You maintain a healthy authority over your child and in doing that help to ensure that you are raising a boy who will respect women when he becomes a man and a girl who will respect men when she becomes a woman. You avoid starting habits that you don't want to continue for the next eighteen years.

175

The more disciplined you are about this, the easier it will actually be on you. For example, if you train your firstborn to stay quietly in bed till you come and get him, you'll earn the right to use the bathroom, brush your teeth, and take care of personal business before you start the long day of being a mother. Your child can learn to look at books or play with toys, but he knows he can't come out until you get him. Can't you see how much easier this will be on you? Imagine how much more energy you'll have—and how, ultimately, you'll probably be a better parent—if you can remain in charge and establish little rituals like these?

Now let's say you don't do this. Let's say you wait until the child screams before you let her out of her crib. What does that tell the kid? *I'm in charge. As soon as I want to get my day started, all I have to do is start screaming and Mom will come running.*

In that household, you'll wake up, tiptoe around the kitchen, maybe choose not to flush the toilet, and very quietly brush your teeth, all because you're afraid of waking up the tiny tyrant. That kid isn't even a year old yet, and already he has you terrified!

"But Dr. Leman, how do I train my child to wait for me to get him out of the crib?"

Get yourself on a schedule, hold to it, and don't give in to crying. It may take up to fourteen days to establish this, but if you stick with it, ultimately junior will get the picture and learn to keep himself busy while you get ready to face the day.

You'll get better at this with the second child. Raising two children at once means that sometimes you have to let some needs go unmet because there's only one of you and two of them. One child may need a diaper change while the other is begging you to make lunch. Well, you can't do both; somebody's going to have to wait.

But with a firstborn, your tendency will be to jump at your child's every request.

Your first instinct is going to be: *How can I stop Madison from crying? If she's crying, it's my job to make her stop!* Later you learn that every baby cries, and you won't allow your baby to manipulate you in this fashion. This can be a hard lesson for some to learn, but it's an essential one. The sooner you put it into practice, the better.

SOCIAL BUNNY?

The tendency for first-time parents is also to try to create a superbaby or supertoddler. You enroll your child in tumbling,

dance class, play groups, and other activities, all in the name
of good physical activity and "socialization."

To me this is sort of like reserving a church for your
daughter's wedding before she's old enough to date. You're
getting way ahead of yourself.

For starters, a young baby needs to learn to bond with her
mom. Bonding isn't something that occurs in two days, two
weeks, or even completely in two years. It's a long process.
The more you strengthen that bond between you and your
child—by doing fun things together, by playing in the park
together, by holding hands with each other—the more you'll
create a lifelong bond.

Kids at two and three years of age are a blast to play with;
they can be very imaginative, they're happy just to have your
attention, and they're small enough for you to pick up and
swing around a bit. When they see a caterpillar for the first
time, you'd think they had discovered gold. And their laughter! Don't you just love to hear a toddler laugh?

177
• • • • •

All too soon your child is going to enter preschool or
kindergarten and develop other friends outside your family
circle. Instead of playing with your child, you'll be watching
your child play with someone else. But there's no reason to
hurry this process along—and many good reasons to delay it.

Between three and three-and-a-half years of age, I think
it's healthy to get your child involved with other kids. That's
why there are benefits to preschool. But if you decide not to
enroll your child in preschool, don't feel like you're a rotten
parent or worry that you'll have a socially inept child.
Nobody my age went to preschool, and we (at least most of
us) seem to be doing just fine.

Many parents—even other experts—talk as if your child
will be an outcast for life if you don't start them early in a
variety of programs to stretch their bodies, minds, and social

skills. But I don't see much benefit in going out of your way to effect "socialization" prior to three years of age. Oh, there will be the times when your infant or toddler is in the church nursery, or your best friend comes to visit and she has a little one close in age to your child. But play groups and play experiences are, in my opinion, vastly overrated. For infants and children up to age three, I'm far more concerned about what is happening between parent and child than I am about how "social" a two-and-a-half-year-old appears.

So resist this trend—and you and your baby will be better off in the long run. By all means, don't sign your two-year-old up for gymnastics because you're worried that she doesn't seem to be very good playing with other kids. That's too much, too soon, too quick. Your child will have plenty of time to socialize with other kids. And the success of that socialization will depend in large part upon your child's bond with you, not experiences of being with other kids under the age of three.

Just wait. Besides, by the time your daughter is thirteen, she'll be so social it'll drive you crazy. Every time you pick up the phone you'll have to suffer through two girls giggling away about the "dork" they saw that day in gym class.

I realize that much of what I'm saying goes against the current tide of popular opinion, but I hope you'll stand up for it. Tell you what—I'll make you a deal. Drive into your average preschool parking lot. If you'll give me a five-dollar bill for every SUV and minivan in the parking lot, I'll give you a twenty-dollar bill for every other kind of car. Who do you think will come out ahead on that one? I bet I will, by far. You know why? Because we humans tend to act like clones. We watch what others are doing and then do the same thing. It's part of our human longing for connection, for acceptance. But sometimes "the same thing" isn't a good thing.

In this day and age we worry far too much about prematture socialization and far too little about parent-child bonding. A healthy child does not need to be around other children before he or she turns three, but a healthy child does need round-the-clock care from a loving parent. But we Americans sometimes turn these important philosophies around— putting children in all-day care and preschools while moms and dads both go off and do their own thing. This thinking is backwards, and it's past the time when we need to resist it.

Socialization, of course, is the main critique leveled at homeschoolers. But I marvel at what many of these parents are able to pull off. Sande and I didn't homeschool our children, but I see a number of benefits for some families to pursue this. The worst argument against homeschooling is the "socialization" one, which I don't think is really an issue at all.

179

At its root, the rush to socialize our children denies the full impact that we can have as parents. Don't sell yourself short; you can make a tremendous difference in your kid's life. Encouraging and loving words, tactile stimulation, laughing together, reading together, having meals together, and creating an overall sense of belonging are ten times more important than putting two toddlers together on the same playground for one hour and calling it "socialization."

MAKE MEMORIES!

People who come to me for therapy don't remember anything about playing with kids when they were two years old. They don't speak fondly of being driven around town between gymnastics, Girl Scouts, ballet, and soccer. But they do remember family dinners, Friday-night family

Yahtzee games, and homemade apple pies cooling in the kitchen—or the lack of them.

These types of memories are far more profound, long lasting, and healthy than giving your toddler a frantic childhood. Do you really want your child to remember a mom who was always looking harried and acting stressed, or who was always talking to herself or on the cell phone as she tried to keep up with an overly busy schedule, worried that she's running ten minutes late? Do you really think that helps your child?

Slow down. Get to know and bond with your child. Live a disciplined life. Establish a healthy authority. If you can do these four things, your child will go into toddlerhood and come out of toddlerhood with a strong character, a foundation of belonging, and a very high chance of maturing into a healthy, caring, and mature adult.

10

Tricks of the Trade

To be forewarned is to be forearmed. I want to equip you with full knowledge of six of the most common tactics little kids use to get your attention or to get their own way. After decades of doing family counseling, I've found that few kids are truly original. So take comfort: Whatever your child is doing has almost certainly been done many times before. You just need to learn your firstborn's "tricks of the trade" and how best to respond to them.

BITING

There's a church in Tucson, Arizona, whose door my wife will never darken again. We took Hannah there when she was young enough to stay in the nursery. Some kid took a chomp out of her hat and actually left teeth marks on her head. Unfortunately, this isn't all that uncommon. A University of Minnesota study found that almost half of the 224 kids enrolled in a daycare center were bitten at least once over a one-year period.

Little kids bite, particularly around the ages of three or four. Some do it aggressively, some do it innocently, and some do it playfully. But no matter the motivation, it's a behavior that you want to stop right away.

Why do kids bite? Good question. If we knew the definitive answer to that question, we might develop better strategies to stop it. But I have to confess that this is one of the more difficult character issues I've ever counseled on. My guess is that a lot of kids' biting has more to do with their teething; chomping down on something, even if it's human flesh, helps them feel better for a second or two. Other kids might bite as a sign of anger, frustration, or aggression. Some kids just want attention, and they've learned that the horrified response to biting brings a lot of attention. Others might see something dangling in front of them and chomp down out of curiosity, almost forgetting that there's a person attached to those dancing fingers.

Once again, it helps to know your child's motivation as you consider how best to address this behavior. Experts are all over the map on how to handle this problem. Some will tell you to bite back, and for what it's worth, I've had a lot of parents tell me they've bitten their kids back and that has stopped any such behavior immediately. But I can't make that recommendation to you as a psychologist. For starters, if you break the skin, you can pass a nasty infection onto your kid. Also, you're going to have a very difficult time explaining that mark to any DCFS (Department of Children and Family Services) worker.

I suggest you say a very firm "No!" Shake your finger as you say this, and then immediately remove your child from the scene. Isolate him for one or two minutes, which will seem like an eternity to a two-year-old. When junior learns that biting means being isolated, he's likely to think twice before he bites again.

Keep in mind, little Jessica isn't born with a fully developed self-control mechanism. You have to take the time to teach her that there are right ways and wrong ways to respond to others' aggression. You can use words, you can walk away, you can turn around, but you shouldn't bite.

This type of conversation assumes a certain maturity, which is another reason why I don't see the need to socialize kids who are younger than three years old. Kids younger than three are likely to act on their impulses, and they lack the ability to understand your reasoned explanations.

HOLDING THEIR BREATH

Younger children, particularly those three and under, soon discover how fearful Mom and Dad can be of any potential medical emergency. Particularly when a mother or father overreacts to a minor injury, little Buford quickly grasps how this fear can be turned to his advantage. Feeling powerless, he decides to take charge. *Oh yeah,* he says to himself, *I've got your number. If you won't let me get my way, I'm going to stop breathing.*

This can terrify a concerned first-time parent, particularly when the child turns red or even blue. Unfortunately, some mothers become so frightened that they immediately give in. *Denying him a cookie isn't worth dying for,* they think—but their motivation for giving the child that cookie couldn't be more off base.

Though this is a popular kid trick, it's a paper tiger. A child can't hurt herself by holding her breath. Even if your child is unusual and is able to make herself pass out, as soon as she does so, she'll start to breathe again.

Your best antidote is to ignore the behavior or say something like, "Boy, that must really be getting uncomfortable;

but you're still not getting your way," and then walk away. The only power this tactic will have is the power you let it have by giving it any attention. Read that sentence again— because it's the key to stopping any unwanted behavior in your child.

WHINING

You know your best defense against whining? Build a whine cellar! I'm not kidding. Maybe it's more economical for you to designate a room for this purpose, but the idea is that once you put your child in a place where you can't hear him, the whining can't and won't continue.

Whining inevitably arises when your child is old enough to talk back and is either forbidden from doing something he wants to do or told he has to do something he doesn't want to do. Everybody will be happier if you nip whining in the bud. When you try to "talk through" a whining session, you reinforce the unwanted behavior by paying it attention. When two-year-old Melissa kicks the door and your response is, "Melissa Jane, stop kicking that door!" what does Melissa do?

Kick, kick, kick, kick.

Many first-time parents make a big mistake here by adding, "Melissa, didn't I tell you not to kick that door? Why are you kicking that door?"

Kick, kick.

"Melissa! If you kick that door one more time, you're really going to get it!"

Kick, kick, kick, kick, kick.

Melissa is getting exactly what she wants: your attention. If you allow your children to do something three times before you warn "one more time," they'll pick up that they get to do something four times before they really have to stop. The same thing happens with whining.

Here's a scenario:

> "But Mom, I don't want to go to Brandon's house today; he's boring."
> "Honey, Brandon's mom is my best friend and we're going."
> "But couldn't we go to the park instead?"
> "No, we're going to Brandon's."
> "How 'bout if we go to the pool? Don'cha wanna go to the pool?"
> "Sweetie, I already told Brandon's mom that we were going over there."
> "But I don't want to go to Brandon's house. Why can't we just stay home?"

185
• • • • •

All of this conversation is unnecessary. If you don't want to reinforce a negative behavior, don't respond to it. Remove yourself from the situation. Don't give any indication that the behavior has the slightest chance of being tolerated—or that it could possibly succeed in getting the child what he wants. You are not obligated to explain your actions to a two-year-old!

Some mothers go through this scenario, and then tell me, "Dr. Leman, I never give in. But he still whines all the time. How come?"

Even if Buford knows you won't give in, if he's strong-willed (and as I stated earlier, what child isn't?) he's going to try to make you pay for making him visit Brandon. Oh, he knows it's inevitable that he's going to boring Brandon's house today, but he thinks that if he can make your entire morning miserable, you'll think twice about ever making him go to Brandon's house again. In other words, he's punishing you for taking him to Brandon's house and is trying to shape *you!* Are you going to let him—or are you in charge?

How do you stop whining? Well, how do you stop a fish from swimming? You take the fish out of water! Keep a firm line, put the kid in a place where you can't hear, see, or respond to his guerilla tactics, and then walk away. Remove his audience, and the actor has to stop.

Use your brain here. If you yell back, "I can't hear you!" little Buford knows you can hear him, or you wouldn't be saying it. But if you go to the other side of the house, put on some music, and really do focus on something else, he'll get the picture that his whining is falling on deaf ears.

TABLETOP MASSACRES

Let's suppose you've read everything we've talked about so far with great interest. You preserve family time around the dinner table. You're eager for quality interaction with your kid. And then one night, a tabletop massacre erupts. Food goes flying, the kid is screaming, you get that "I've lost and being a parent is just impossible" look on your face, and the entire evening seems shot.

Not every kid will lead you into these episodes, but many will. You might have three children who behave like guppies at the dinner table—quietly eating their meal, hardly making a sound, leaving almost no mess. But maybe you also got a piranha. He throws food. He kicks his high-chair tray. He drops his dishes on the floor and then claps his hands with delight!

What's really going on—and what can you do about it?

Determine your child's motivation.

First, you have to determine your piranha's motivation. Some kids do goofy things at the dinner table out of curiosity. What you see as food, he sees as a dozen different sensations: *These mashed potatoes feel really mushy in my hands—I wonder what they would feel like in my hair? And wow, that corn is yellow! Look at the way it flies. Hooo weeee! That one landed in the sugar bowl! Maybe I can get this one in the butter! Look at how those pureed carrots make such fascinating shapes when you pour them out. Cool! The shape keeps changing! This is far out!*

How do you determine if this is curiosity or rebellion? In time you'll just be able to tell. If you know your kid, you know what's behind his thinking. Check his attitude. Is he smiling or scowling? Does he honestly seem to be exploring, or is he trying to use negative behavior to get your attention? I don't think you should punish curious infants.

Set realistic expectations.

Second, many first-time parents simply expect way too much of their toddlers, particularly at mealtime. Children don't sit for forty-five minutes while you have an adult conversation about the economy. If you expect to bring a toddler into a restaurant, with all kinds of new sounds and smells and sights, and expect him to ignore everything, remain quiet for an hour or more, and behave like an adult, you're just not being realistic.

If you really want to enjoy your evening out, leave baby with your parents or a close friend. Don't put your child in a situation where 90 percent of babies will fail. Yes, this means you're going to have to limit your activities for a while, but that doesn't mean you can't go out to eat—it just means you should do so on a date rather than as an entire family.

Related to this is the whole Disney phenomenon. Okay, I

187
. . . . .

complained about this earlier in the book, but just give me a moment's leeway to get on my soapbox again (with no offense to Disney's Magic Kingdom). Why parents take young toddlers to Disneyland or Disney World, I'll never know. And why they expect their toddlers to last for more than three or four hours is absolutely beyond me. If you must go on an expensive vacation with a young toddler, get a several-days pass and expect to leave the park early every day. Toddlers are not designed to remain peaceful and cooperative and quiet when their nap schedule is broken, their eating schedule is blasted with treats and popcorn and sugary drinks, and their little minds are overstimulated with rides, sights, sounds, and constant music. In fact, if you take your toddler through "It's a Small World," you might as well pack it up right there! She's seen enough for at least a day with all those sights, sounds, and that everlasting, annoying, refusing-to-be-forgotten song!

Every time I've been in the Magic Kingdom, I've seen moms who look exhausted and miserable, kids who are overwhelmed and crying, and discouraged dads who are mentally calculating that this miserable vacation is costing them about five hundred dollars a day. Listen very carefully: Children have limits. Exceed those limits—even on vacation—at your own peril. If your child is overly tired, she's going to fuss and cry and whine. It doesn't matter if she's in Disneyland, at a fancy restaurant, or a birthday party at Chuck E. Cheese's. Tired kids fall apart.

If you've bonded with your child, you'll soon know the look in her eyes that will tell you when dinner is over. Before there's an eruption or a mess, remove that child from the high-chair, and save yourself the hassle of trying to mop up the kitchen floor, walls, and ceiling.

SLEEPING ROUTINES

This is a very common concern. When a mom approaches me about this, I begin by giving her some basic background information.

Set a routine you can live with for a long time.

Most children have a routine. Your job is to shape that routine and then hold to it. The problem is, by the time most parents come to me, the routine is already set and they have to change it. That's a bit more difficult to do, but it's still possible.

Even though you're now dealing with your firstborn, I want to give you a heads-up on child number two, if such a child comes along: Don't expect her to have the same routine. She won't. Every one of our five kids has been vastly different about their going-to-bed routine. Child number four, for example, had to have her "weebie" before she went to bed. Somewhere along the way, Hannah ended up with a square cutout of one of Sande's old slips. She just loved the feel of that slip against her cheek; it was so soft and shiny that she needed it every time we laid her down for bed. Sande eventually got some edging and turned that slip into a sort of blanket, but we still called it a "weebie." Why did we call it a "weebie," you may ask? Because that's what Hannah started calling it when she was two years old! (Your family will make up lots of words—just call it your own family vocabulary. Some of which, of course, can't be shared with outsiders or with your child's dates down the road.)

Now child number one, Holly, had several blankets she liked to choose from to sleep with, so part of her routine was picking out a blanket. I recommend that you try to find one thing that your child likes to sleep with and stay with that. The more things they have to choose from, the more they can draw out bedtime as they ponder their decision. I've

189

heard of some toddlers who will take forty-five minutes to choose which animal or doll they want to sleep with that night. Don't fall for this! Give your child thirty seconds, and then say, "If you don't choose one, Mommy is going to choose for you." Warning: If you say this, follow through with it, and don't back down. You'll save yourself a lot of grief in the future when your child learns that you mean what you say at bedtime.

Once you get into your routine—brushing her teeth, reading a story, choosing her doll or blankie, kissing her cheek, saying a prayer—may God have mercy on your soul if you leave out one step, especially with a firstborn. This is why I recommend that the simpler your routine is, the better it'll be for both you and your child. You may be able to spend sixty minutes putting your kid to bed on most days, but as life gets more complex, that sixty-minute routine is going to come back to haunt you. And if you try to trim it down to forty-five minutes, you'll spend another half-hour trying to explain why you're not going through the normal one!

Stick to your routine like glue!

Why is it so difficult to get some firstborns down at night? For starters, they don't have a brother or sister who also has to go to bed. From the firstborn's perspective, he is the only one in the entire family who has to go to bed early, and how is that fair?!

Second, your child is thinking, *It's so much fun to be with Mommy and Daddy. I feel so safe, and if I need anything, all I have to do is fuss or cry and they're right there!* Now, why would that child ever want to go to a dark room all by himself where Mommy and Daddy won't hear every little hiccup and come running at the slightest sound of distress?

It took me a couple children to catch on to the power of

routine. Our true firstborn, Holly, was a great pointer and grunter—how stupid we were back then! I let her direct me as if I were a two-hundred-pound marionette. Our hall couldn't have been more than twenty feet long, but Holly could stretch that walk out for a good fifteen minutes.

Have you ever made a snowman with wet snow? There's nothing better because the snow is so easy to pick off the grass that it leaves a clear path of green behind it. That's what Holly was like on her way to bed—a snowball rolling through wet snow. We'd walk by a bear and she'd go, "Uh, uh, uh, uh!" until I stooped down to pick up the bear. Then she'd want a pillow, a toy, a blankie— anything that we passed if stopping for it could add another ten seconds to the routine. Everything was sucked up into my arms on the way to bed. Before long Holly's crib looked like *Sanford and Son*'s junkyard, and there was no room for Holly. And good luck trying to take one little thing out of her bed to make room for her!

191
• • • • •

Here's a simple question that can make your life so much easier. When I've used it with harried moms, I can see the tension drain out of their face when they recognize what I'm saying. Ask yourself this: "Do I really want to be subject to my child's demands for the rest of my life?"

If your answer is yes, there's nothing I can do for you! Prepare to be a miserable doormat for the rest of your life.

But if your answer is no, then begin now by helping your child establish a very simple and concise routine for bedtime. Remember: You're the mommy. You're in charge. If you act like things will always be that way, your child will fall into line. If she thinks she can argue or direct her way out of bed, or at least delay bedtime for another hour, she'll never stop.

The danger is when you're really tired (another reason to seriously reconsider working long hours while raising your kids). If out of weariness you give in to one grunt to avoid a confrontation that you just don't have the strength to face, why in the world would your kid think it's going to be any different the next night? Children are natural masters of the game of manipulation.

So work hard to develop a very simple routine, and stick to it. Your child might fuss the first night or two, but if you don't give in to his cries, you're laying the groundwork for years of much easier good-nights.

TEMPER TANTRUMS

What I'm about to say is going to sound so unconventional and so against the grain of modern thinking that you may be tempted to dismiss it outright. But please hang with me: Just because your child is unhappy is not a good enough reason for you to rearrange your life to make things easier for her.

If you don't believe this, you're setting yourself up for some major power struggles with your child. If you think your son or daughter's happiness is the most important thing in the world, you'll crumble as soon as she stomps her feet, screams and yells, and tells everyone just how unhappy she is.

In order for your child to mature emotionally, relationally, and socially, she must realize she is not the center of the universe. The message you want to convey is this: *You're important, loved, and prized, but there are other people who count in life besides yourself.*

If you raise self-centered sons or daughters, they will never have a happy marriage. They will forever be fighting with people at work. And they will be frustrated for their entire lives. The best gift you can give to your future son- or daughter-in-law is a spouse who has learned to put other people first.

What I've just said has everything to do with responding to a young toddler's temper tantrums. First and foremost, a temper tantrum is a major power struggle, a child's attempt to lay down the gauntlet and say, *Just how far are you willing to go to deny me what I want?* Whining (which we talked about earlier in this chapter) is the first stage of this power struggle; the tantrum is the ultimatum.

Your response should be similar to what you did with whining:

Walk away.

First, sidestep the power struggle by walking away from it. In no way should you allow your child to think that this behavior will garner any attention or concern from you. You must completely remove all motivation for your toddler to behave in this manner. Simply step over her as she kicks and screams on the floor and walk away. Don't negotiate: "If you don't stop kicking and screaming, I'm going to put you in your room. . . ." Your child needs to learn that she should not expect to debate her mother, who is twenty-five years older than she is and much wiser. Your child also needs to realize that certain forms of communication will not be tolerated, especially temper tantrums.

Stay calm.

Second, be calm, say things once with a firm *no*, and if you can't leave the scene, pick the child up and remove her from the scene. She needs to learn that it's not your job to meet every conceivable need that she might have. Sometimes we can't do what we want to do because others are busy with other things. Even a mother can't drop everything just to satisfy her firstborn.

Think "down the road."

If things get tense and your will starts to weaken, just imagine the impact a wise parent can have in this situation. If your

193

firstborn becomes CEO of a large company, thousands of employees will be grateful that you have confronted the selfish, hard-driving, run-over-people mentality that frequently adorns out-of-control firstborns. If your child becomes a government official, he will have learned that people aren't pawns to be used and discarded, but they have their own needs too.

Though it sounds like a cliché in this pop-psychology age, my goal here is to empower you. I want you to develop parent power. You must assume a position of authority over your child. We as humans will destroy ourselves if we never learn to deny some of our wants.

By teaching your child that all his wants can't be met, you're doing him a great service. I love doughnuts, but my nutritionist friend Pam Smith tells me that doughnuts are one of the worst things I could ever have for breakfast. I've had to learn to deny myself those culinary confections and severely limit my intake—even though I like them and wouldn't mind eating them five days a week!

Don't let your child call the shots.

In my book *Making Children Mind without Losing Yours*, I talk about a little tyke who had a tantrum at the mall, on the floor, in front of God and 1,500 strangers. The mother was mortified, embarrassed, ashamed. She was being gawked at, and she could swear that her child knew exactly what he was doing.

What should you do in that situation? Step over the child (not *on* the child—resist that temptation!) and walk away.

Oh, this is great, Dr. Leman, I can imagine some of you thinking. *What are you going to do with the dozens of people who are watching?*

That's easy. Just shake your head and say out loud, "Some people's children . . ."

That tyke will get up, flailing his arms all the way, and run after you. You won't lose him.

You must understand the psychology behind this situation. What your child is essentially saying is this: *Listen, Mom, you're going to do what I want you to do. I'm aware that people are watching, so I'm going to use them as a power base to make sure you succumb to my demands for sugar. I want sugar. You give me ice cream, or you give me a sucker, or you give me a cookie because if I don't get sugar right now, I'm going to embarrass you in front of all these people. I don't care if you've got a healthy lunch planned at home that we'll be eating in thirty minutes. I want sugar, and I want it now.*

195
· · · · ·

Believe it or not, when your child acts this way, he has just given you a great gift. He is giving you the opportunity to show him that when you say no, you *mean* no. If he wants to make a fool of himself in front of strangers, he can go right ahead. He can claim to be in charge, or at least play to gain the upper hand, but if you remain firm, calm, and collected, he's toast. Your gift to him is to say and show him, "As the parent, I'm in authority over you. I understand that you want sugar, but I know what's best for you. We're going to eat a healthy lunch at home."

I don't want to scare you, but just about every parent has been in at least one extremely embarrassing public episode with their child. I can't promise that some bystanders won't judge you or look down at you (just wait till they have their own children, and then they'll know!). But if you handle yourself with a calm, firm, and authoritative manner, the wise shoppers will respect you and even be rooting for you. If you truly want to make yourself look pathetic, just give in—

then everybody will see firsthand how weak you are and really will, with some justification, judge you.

This is more than just my opinion. No less an authority than the apostle Paul himself said, "Children, obey your parents."[6] When your child is between the ages of two and three, you're going to face at least a couple of these battles. Your child will try to test your authority. You mustn't allow a child to call the shots in your household. Once you give a firstborn the reins, she will never let go. She'll drive you for the rest of your life.

Not long ago I was traveling through the Dallas-Fort Worth airport, sitting at a food court, when a three-year-old girl let everybody within a two-block radius know that she wanted a Happy Meal. Mom said no, and the daughter brazenly slapped her mother in the face.

Grandma, who was seated with the mother and her daughter, looked on in horror. She was clearly mortified by her granddaughter's behavior, but seemingly more so with the mom's actions! You could see the words she so wanted to say: "Are you going to take that?" Not only did the mom take it, to make things worse, she actually got up and bought her daughter a Happy Meal! I had to fight every impulse within me to get up and explain to this weak-willed parent what she was getting herself into.

Part of me will never understand how we adults can let a little person shorter than a yardstick call the shots. Kids catch on pretty quickly. They feel the power in public places, knowing they have an audience, sensing their parent's fear, intuitively picking up that this is where their parents are most vulnerable. Even a three-year-old knows when she has Mom around her little finger.

If your kid is going through this stage, be ready at any time to simply walk out of the store. Yeah, you may have a cart full of groceries. But so what? Simply tell the manager, "Sorry, but I've got to deal with a discipline problem here." He'll understand. You may not have finished shopping for the clothes you needed to buy or the gift you needed to pick out, but the stakes of the current situation are so high that anything else can wait.

Don't give in. Once you yield power to your child in this manner, you're going to have a real battle on your hands. The sooner you make your child understand that you will never lay down your authority to a kid who still messes in his pants, the better!

If you've left the store and your kid is still kicking and screaming, find some nice soft music on the stereo, turn the speakers forward, crank up the volume, and tune your child out. It's best to say nothing until the child has quieted down. For starters, you're probably embarrassed, angry, and tired yourself, and that's not the best state of mind to be in when you're administering discipline. And second, your child isn't hearing what you have to say anyway. She's still fighting, and you must teach her that you won't debate, you won't shout over her shouts, and that this behavior will never get her the attention or power that she craves.

If your little girl goes to sleep before you get home, thank God for small favors and put her down for a nap. Don't worry about changing her diaper, feeding her, or anything like that. Don't revive her; just let her sleep. Your primary act of discipline has already been done—your child threw a tantrum, and what did she get out of it? Nothing.

If she does wake up, or if she finally quiets down, say with a tone of authority, "Honey, what went on at Kmart isn't okay. Mommy doesn't like that; you have to do what I say without complaining." As you speak these words, give her "the look" of disapproval. Your child needs to see you being firm. "When Mommy says no, Mommy means no. That type of behavior will never get me to change my mind."

This is not the time to go into a huge conversation about how God doesn't want her to act that way, or how Jesus is watching her, or anything like that. In the aftermath, keep it bare bones simple: That kind of behavior is never going to get the result you want. *Ever.*

When you refuse to give in, when you resist all attempts at negotiating or debating, your child realizes a couple of very healthy things. First, she realizes that Mom has a mind and a will of her own; she can't be manipulated or controlled. Second, she learns that no one member of the family is more important than any other member of the family. Firstborns in particular seem to have the hardest time learning this last lesson, but it's a vital one.

198

THIS CASINO IS RIGGED

Temper tantrums and the like are such an intense topic that it's no wonder parents get a little overwhelmed. But relax. The only power your toddler has is the power you *choose* to give him. Think about it: You're stronger, you're smarter, you're more experienced, you can read books to increase your wisdom, and you have the ability to get counsel from others. Your child has none of that. All he has is the power to embarrass you or make your life miserable. Since you have the ability to walk away, you can remove his most powerful weapon.

In other words, this casino is rigged—you can win every time. You don't need to fear your child. You don't even need to struggle with your child. You can sidestep it all the way! Don't negotiate, don't argue. Just be the full-grown parent you already are.

You have the power. Use it.

11

The Birds and the Bees

"Dr. Leman," you're saying, "we're talking about babies and toddlers here, and you want to bring up sex? Are you serious?"

I couldn't be more serious. Believe it or not, sex is a reality even for infants—not in the way it is for grown-ups, of course, but we humans learn very early on that certain parts of our bodies are more pleasurable to touch than others. Sexual awakening is something that occurs as a process, and that process begins when we're still in diapers.

First-time parents who try to pretend this isn't so will be caught off-guard when they notice their child's early fascination with their genitals. I worked with one mother who was petrified because she caught her four-year-old daughter doing a makeshift "bump and grind" with a pillow in front of the television set one evening.

"Is there something wrong with her?" she asked me.

Let me allay those fears. William Friedrich at the Mayo Clinic studied a thousand children and found that almost all children under the age of five had been observed touching their own genitals. This behavior can begin as early as twelve to eighteen months, and it often peaks around age four.

It's understandable. It feels good to touch our genitals. The fact that this young girl was unconsciously doing the bump and grind shows me that, to her, it was no different from scratching an itch; she was probably finding out by accident that pressure on that part of her body created pleasant sensations. She didn't know that it wasn't appropriate to be doing the bump and grind in the middle of the living room. All she knew was that it felt good.

I told her mom that she should respond without undue alarm or embarrassment, take her daughter into a private place, talk about what had just happened, and explain that certain things are best done in private.

Another mother was startled when she tried to take her three-year-old daughter out of a car seat that had a plastic piece between the child's legs. She noticed that her daughter was rubbing up against her seat, and she quickly tried to take her out. Her daughter protested, "Wait, Mommy, I'm not finished yet."[7]

What happens is that adults look at a situation like this and transfer adult emotions, guilt, motivation, and feelings onto their children. In healthy families, where abuse hasn't occurred, the family and home are the most natural places for kids to learn about their bodies and about sexual feelings—and to do so in an environment that doesn't produce guilt or shame but that teaches morality, responsibility, and appropriate tact.

If your child has been abused sexually in any way, including physical contact and/or being introduced to sexual images that are not age-appropriate, I strongly advise you to seek help from a professional psychologist who shares your faith. Such early experiences can have a lifelong impact on a child and need to be addressed immediately, for the child's and the family's welfare (also see "When Abuse Enters the Picture" in this chapter for further information).

Ignoring your toddler's developing sexuality isn't going to

make it go away. In fact, having healthy and age-appropriate conversations with your children is going to satisfy their curiosity in such a way that they will be less likely to engage in peer-dependent play ("I'll show you mine if you'll show me yours"), and more likely to come to you with future questions.

IT'S NOT A THING

For starters, as soon as your child begins naming body parts, use the correct names for their genitalia. If your first-born is taking a bath, you'd say something like this: "Timmy, that's your elbow. Can you say 'elbow'? That's your knee. Can you say 'knee'? And that's your penis. Can you say 'penis'?"

201
● ● ● ● ●

Your kid isn't as stupid as you might think he is. If you name every body part but one, he's naturally going to catch on that something is . . . well, *different* about this body part. And if you tell Samantha correct names about every organ except her "privates," she's naturally going to think, *Why doesn't this thing here have a "regular" name? There must be something wrong or dirty or unmentionable about it!* This kind of ostrich-sticking-your-head-in-the-sand parenting is where inappropriate guilt and shame come from.

If your child grows up talking to you about these matters, you'll have a much easier time addressing them in the later years. Your kids won't grow up thinking that certain subjects are "off limits." They won't immediately attach embarrassment to their body. They'll be used to talking to you about everything. Doesn't that sound nice?

Early communication and accurate information are also effective tools to help guard your child against exploitation. When you use correct names and talk about body parts, it's natural to say that these particular body parts are not for public display. "Michael, it's okay to be naked in the bathtub or when you're changing in your room. But when you go outside, you need to make sure your penis and your bottom are covered. Those are private."

Girls will notice, and understandably ask, why Dad can go to the beach without a shirt but Mom never does. A simple explanation like this will clear up any confusion and keep the communication lines open: "Honey, women develop breasts. No, you don't have any yet, but you see where your nipples are? Someday you'll develop breasts just like Mommy. And when you do, you need to keep them private. Breasts are something we shouldn't show in public."

You see what I'm doing? Without being embarrassed, I'm using matter-of-fact language, giving accurate information without the emotional overtones that our culture tends to attach to sexual issues. And once I've done this, I have a context in which to say, "No one except perhaps your doctor when your mommy is present should touch you here, Molly. It's okay if Mommy or Daddy are helping you to clean yourself, but you shouldn't allow another adult or friend to play with these parts of your body, okay? They are private."

THE END OF INNOCENCE

When you first bring baby home, nothing is private. You're changing his diaper seven to ten times a day, so your boy is spread-eagled in front of you in all his glory. When he gets hungry, you open your shirt and give him a breast. This is natural and healthy and a part of life.

You may also find that one of the easiest ways to get kids to take a bath is for one of the parents to get in the water with them. As a young parent, I remember taking baths with my two oldest daughters. They sat behind me and I pretended like I was squishing them, which of course would make them squeal. I'd then pretend like I forgot they were there, knowing that it was just a matter of time before a cup of cold water got poured all over my head.

There's a time, however, when that type of activity is no longer appropriate. If in doubt, go on the modest side. Usually one or the other spouse has a different take about modesty levels, and you're probably best off by going with the most conservative spouse's gut feeling on this. When kids are three or four, they don't know too much and won't notice much, but certainly by age five you really need to start toning it down.

When a mom starts asking me about this, I like to tell her that her question is her answer. The mere fact that she's growing uncomfortable with being naked in front of her child tells me that the time has come for her to cover up. If you feel uncomfortable undressing in front of your child, then don't. Build some boundaries in your home. Teach your children that they shouldn't come into your bedroom until they knock, and then model that by doing the same thing when you want to enter their bedroom or bathroom.

But please, don't make the mistake that so many parents make at this stage. They undress in front of their child, let their child walk around naked, and then reach an arbitrary date where this isn't allowed and then lower the boom. Take the time to train your child with gentle teaching, and gradually work into appropriate modesty. Instant admonishing isn't training; your child is moving from full exposure to appropriate privacy. Intuitively, he senses that this is a "step back," access wise, and may resent it—especially if he sees child number two getting to bathe with you or nurse at night.

NORMAL SEX PLAY

Kids won't just be curious about their bodies; they are going to be curious about their friends' bodies as well. The answer is not to keep our kids in the dark but to find appropriate ways to discuss basic anatomy.

If you catch your toddler in a situation where she or he is looking at another child's genitals, or maybe even touching them, don't overreact. As frightening as it can be to adults, that's fairly normal activity. However, that doesn't mean this is activity you want to condone. Calmly pull your child aside, explain what is appropriate and what is not, and use the moment as a time to teach, rather than to yell or overreact.

"Jessica, the body is God's creation, and God tells us that we shouldn't let someone else touch our private body parts like that unless we're married to them."

Curiosity-based sexual play is not an early indicator of a sexual predator or any particular sexual orientation. Some kids are just more curious than others. Be very careful about coloring a toddler's actions with adult motivations.

If the touching wasn't consensual, it becomes a bit more serious. You should have a frank talk with the other child's parents. If your child was the one forcing things along, you're going to have to set out clear guidelines for appropriate behavior. If the inappropriate behavior continues, you should seek counseling.

How can you find out who was "consenting" and who was pushing the envelope? Just ask! Kids at this age tend to be rather open and honest, provided the parent doesn't appear to be panicking or freaking out. If you can maintain your composure long enough to ask what is really going on, the children will most likely give you a pretty accurate account of what took place.

When baby number two comes along, you can use diaper changing as an opportunity to, in a healthy way, have some of these discussions. Helping with the diaper change will answer some of your firstborn's natural curiosity. There are also picture books, written for children, that you may consider using. My wife, Sande, loves the book *Mommy Laid an Egg,* by Babette Cole.

FANCY-FREE

Young children still have their heads in fantasy half the time; as you train them to respect their body and other kids' bodies, remember that all sorts of interpretations can go on in their heads. This is why I so strongly suggest giving very accurate and age-appropriate information.

I was at a friend's house once, and they had a young boy who was going through this fanciful stage. His parents had talked to him about the importance of locking the bathroom door and respecting privacy, but apparently didn't get explicit enough as to why he was supposed to lock the door.

Midway through the evening I needed to use the bathroom. Unfortunately the house had just one, and the door was locked. I waited five minutes or so and rechecked the door. It was still locked, and it seemed really quiet in there. I went back out into the living room and started counting heads.

Everyone was accounted for.

By now, my need was more than arbitrary; it was becoming critical. Someone had locked the bathroom door, and I needed to get in.

Being the psychologist that I am, I noticed a little boy's face and saw the answer written all over it.

"Andy, were you in the bathroom?" I asked.

"No," he said.

"Did you lock the door?" I asked.

"Yes," he admitted.

"Why did you lock the door? Is someone in there?"

"Yes."

"Who?"

"The big bad wolf is in there. Mommy said I have to keep it locked."

We managed to get the door open, and after taking care of my business, I shared my conversation with Andy's mom; she thought it was so funny. It certainly does point out the need to understand that this world is a big and confusing place to little kids. They'll take a story they just heard, a snippet from a conversation, and put all kinds of things together.

That's why training, particularly in this area, needs to be seen as a gentle process. I don't like the notion of "the talk," because one talk is never sufficient. Sexuality is too big an issue to try and summarize in one conversation. Ideally, you'll have an ongoing dialogue with your child throughout your child's life, gradually becoming more explicit as your child ages.

Begin early and appropriately. Model good behavior, and you'll be well on your way to raising a healthy, sexually well-adjusted child.

WHEN ABUSE ENTERS THE PICTURE

As much as any of us hates talking about abuse, it's a sad and ugly part of a sinful world. Children are abused physically, emotionally, verbally, and sexually every day across our country. For the purposes of this chapter on the birds and the bees, we'll talk only about sexual abuse.

Sexual abuse includes any touching inside the bathing suit

areas by someone who has no business doing the touching. It includes showing age-inappropriate images or engaging in age-inappropriate conversations. Any discussions of sexuality with a young child by anyone other than a parent are inappropriate.

It's important to make a distinction about different types of touching so you don't cause confusion: "Honey, it's okay when your mommy or daddy touch you when they are giving you a bath, or for the doctor to touch you when he's giving you a physical exam. Mommy's in the room then, so you know that's okay. That kind of touching is necessary.

"But nobody—not an uncle, brother, family friend, teacher, anybody—should touch you in areas your bathing suit covers. If they try to, I want you to tell Mommy about it right away. If they threaten you about telling, don't worry. You tell me anyway, and I'll make sure you're safe."

Personally, I believe a talk like this is less important than protecting your child. I realize this is controversial, but hear me out. I believe you should *never* place your child in any situation where there is even the remotest chance of this type of activity taking place. Some parents recklessly allow their child to stay in places they haven't thoroughly checked out.

I wouldn't leave our kids with any babysitter I didn't trust to the core. I wouldn't leave them in a church setting if there weren't appropriate checks and balances—an open area, no secret corners, and trustworthy care. I just wouldn't. And if I had any suspicions at all about any relatives, they wouldn't get in the same room with my child, much less be alone with her.

If I do my job, the chances of one of my children being molested go way, way down. It's when we allow children to roam free or put them in situations where they aren't watched appropriately that trouble arises. Give me one good

207
• • • • •

reason your three- or four-year-old should be anywhere without parental supervision! I can't think of one!

I hear of some parents who organize sleepovers for five-year-old children. There's no way you'll find a Leman at one of those things. As a counselor, I've heard the stories. Do you realize what you provide to a married pedophile (and a lot of pedophiles *are* married) when you fill a house with five-year-old girls? Haven't you heard about the cameras, not to mention physical acts that are even worse?

If your child is too young to fend for herself, she's too young to be in a situation where she's vulnerable. You can't ask a five-year-old to match wits with a fifty-year-old man, so don't put your child in that situation.

If, despite your best efforts, abuse does occur, you have to bring in a professional who has worked with kids in this area. I wish I could give you five quick steps, but it would be bordering on malpractice for me to do that, and the context of this book isn't the appropriate place anyway. A thorough discussion of this topic would warrant at least a chapter, if not an entire book.

So, in a nutshell, here's my advice: Have a short talk with your child, but focus even more on preventive care. Never place any of your children in a situation where there is the remotest possibility of sexual molestation.

YOUR GOAL

When did you first learn about sexuality? If you're like 90 percent of us, you learned about sex in a situation surrounded by guilt. Maybe you were abused. Maybe you shared a "dirty" book that got passed around among school friends. Maybe you had ideas that were just plain silly and you laugh about them now.

The percentage of children who get healthy, accurate, and age-appropriate information about sexuality from their parents is ridiculously low. Why not decide right now to give such a gift to your son or daughter? Why not let your children benefit from being introduced to sexuality in a healthy, safe, and guilt-free environment?

I've surprised many by teaching that the opposite-sex parent should be the primary sexual educator. Mom, if you have a son, you should be his primary educator in this matter. Dad, if you have a daughter, it's your job to appropriately teach her about the facts of life. There are exceptions—for instance, when it comes to sanitation surrounding a young woman's first period, I think it's only natural for Mom to take the lead. But when it comes to helping a child understand the mysteries of sexuality, who is better than Dad to tell a daughter what a young man is truly thinking on a date? Who is better than Mom to tell a young man that girls don't really think it's cool when a boy tries to impress a girl by making fun of her?

What happens when the same-sex parent does the teaching is that all kinds of inaccurate information get passed down. As a counselor, I can't tell you how many times I've had to swallow a good laugh as a woman described for me the "talk" her mom gave her the night before her wedding.

Your goal is to create a child who is morally chaste but educated and informed, recognizing sex as a wonderful gift from God that is appropriate only within a marriage relationship. Imagine the joy in your heart to think about the day that your young son or daughter is getting married. You know they have kept themselves pure for their wedding night, and you also know they have learned about sex in a guilt-free environment, recognizing it for the God-given gift that it is. This is such a rare and precious treasure for you to give your child, and take it from me—such a great start will help your child avoid many of the most common sexual frustrations within marriage.

This type of training will take time and energy. And you'll have to work through some of your own embarrassment—especially if you grew up in a home where sex or private body parts weren't openly discussed. But if you'll take the challenge, someday your kid is really going to thank you.

12

When the Thing Comes Home
(or Armageddon on Maple Street)

Let's play a game for a second. Let's pretend that your husband comes home tonight and says to you, "Honey, you know I love you beyond measure. I just love you as much as anybody could ever love anybody. In fact, I love you so much that I think I'd like to have two wives. Wouldn't that be wonderful?

"I know you might think I'm talking like a crazy man, but think about it. There's this woman at work. She is so sweet and thoughtful. Everybody loves her, so I know you will too. And her looks! Oh, has she got looks! She has the cutest dimples I have ever seen. And you know how you always said you admired redheads? You'll just love her red hair.

"The two of you can share the housework, you can go shopping together, and when I'm out of town, maybe you can even go to the movies together. Doesn't that sound like fun?"

Your jaw has dropped to the floor, and then your husband asks, "So, honey, what do you think?"

If you are like most women, as soon as your husband started talking like this, you'd be thinking, *So where did he say he stores his rifle?*

Now put yourself in the shoes of a two-and-a-half-year-old firstborn. For almost three years, this little princess has ruled like Her Majesty the Queen. She's had all your attention; she hasn't had to share you with anyone. Besides, she can play with any toys at any time without having to worry about anyone butting in. She kind of likes things the way they are.

But one day you come home and say, "Honey, we love you so much that we've decided to have a second child. Won't that be so much fun? You'll get to have a little brother or sister to play with!"

In her little mind, she's thinking that her primary caregiver has just told her that she's not good enough. I know you haven't said she's not good enough, but that's how your child will interpret it: *Why do they need another kid? They already have me! Aren't I good enough?*

Before you start thinking how silly this is, remember the opening story—if your husband wanted to bring home another wife, wouldn't you think that he was indirectly telling you that you're not enough for him?

Firstborns never outgrow this. One time when Holly was in her twenties, Sande and I took her out for dinner and then the three of us went to a movie together. All evening long, it was just Sande, Holly, and me. We had a great time, and at the end of the evening, Holly looked at us and said, "You know, it should always have been like this."

GETTING BEHIND YOUR CHILD'S EYES

Your first step when breaking the news about the pending arrival of a new sibling, and once again when bringing child number two home from the hospital, is to get behind your firstborn child's eyes. Your child—still less than a yardstick tall and enjoying every inch of life just as it is—is about to receive a curveball high and tight. If not handled properly, you can unleash a skirmish that will make the Cain-and-Abel story look like a day in the park with Mr. Rogers.

Take a step back, imagine what life has been like for your firstborn, and you'll see why I titled this chapter "When the Thing Comes Home." If your firstborn could get onto the Internet, he might be tempted to order one of those novelty doormats I saw once. Instead of proclaiming "Welcome," these mats read, "Go away!" In the mind of your child his home turf is about to be invaded by an alien.

But if we use our heads as parents, we can teach this child how to absorb the "little immigrant" into the family without too much tension. Here are some suggestions to make the transition easier.

213
• • • • •

SPACING

For starters, consider carefully how you want to space your children. I know, I know—reproduction isn't an exact science; you can't always determine when and how frequently you're going to have kids. But as much as it's in your power, as you think about adding to your family, keep in mind that kids who are less than two years apart tend to have more competition between each other. To make matters worse, a mom who has two kids under the age of three is going to be flat out of energy six days out of seven. She's just trying to make it through the day, flopping into bed at night exhausted (only to have her helpful husband say, "Are you feeling as frisky as I am?"). When the secondborn arrives just eighteen to twenty-four months after child number one, it can feel like a double whammy. Mom is just getting her breath back when *boom!* If she's birthing this child, her body is now once again exhausted, literally cooking up an entirely new human being—only now, she's not just pregnant, she's pregnant and has a toddler! If she's adopting this child, her time and energies and emotions are once again tied up in paperwork, the stress of updating her adoption home study, and FBI fingerprinting over lunch, to name just a few of the additional items on her checklist.

That's one of the reasons, quite frankly, that this book is written for first-time moms. By the time child number two comes around, you may not have time to read any books like this. The only books you'll touch may be the books you pick up to throw at the dog who's driving you crazy or any other being who crosses you once too often!

In my view the ideal spacing for children is about three to four years. Some of you might be tempted to ask, "What's the big difference between two years and three years?"

Well, you do the math—the difference between two years and three years between siblings is 50 percent of the older kid's life!

With a three- or four-year gap, it's a little easier to sell the arrival of kid number two. Your firstborn is now older and better able to accept labels such as "big brother" or "big sister" rather than "chief rival."

BREAKING THE NEWS

Different people have different feelings about when to tell the firstborn about the impending arrival of child number two. Some like to wait as long as possible, or at least for the first three months, in case there's a miscarriage, some other difficulty that would be hard to explain, or a change in the paperwork of your chosen child. If you're pregnant, that's a tough secret to keep from an inquisitive toddler who follows you around all day. Such a boy is likely to hear you talking on the phone to your mom or girlfriend, or overhear his mommy and daddy talking in the living room.

When you tell your child is a matter of personal preference, but I do think it's wise, if you're pregnant, to tell your firstborn as soon as you start to show. A visibly pregnant woman will draw all number of comments wherever she goes: "Oh, you're pregnant! When are you due?"

A very friendly stranger might even try to draw your child into the conversation. "Oh, look at that; you're going to have a little brother or sister! Aren't you excited?"

You don't want your kid to find out about such a transition this way, so whatever date you choose, make sure it's before you start to show. And if you're adopting, don't wait until the last day before you share that joy with your child. Make him or her part of the process, even with its ups and downs.

If you're pregnant, you can have a conversation with an older child that goes something like this. You might begin by reading a book about how babies are born, and then say:

"Honey, you know how your friend Laura has a little brother?"
"Yes."
"Well, guess what?"
"What?"
"No, I want you to guess. Something wonderful is going to happen to our family."
"We're going to Disneyland?"
"No, we're not going to Disneyland."
"You're going to buy me a present?"
"No, we're not going to buy you a present, but we are going to get something."
"What?"
"Should I give you a clue?"
"Yes."
"Feel Mommy's tummy." (Take your firstborn's hand

and place it on your stomach.) "Does Mommy's tummy feel like it's getting any bigger?"

"It feels a little harder."

"That's right. Do you know why it's feeling bigger and harder?"

"No."

"Do you think it's because Mommy is growing a pumpkin?"

"No." (The firstborn laughs.)

"Do you think it's because Mommy is growing a watermelon?"

"Noooooo."

"What do you suppose is in Mommy's tummy, growing bigger every day?"

"A baby."

"A baby, you're right! Mommy is going to have a baby. Which means you're going to have a little brother or a little sister."

If you're adopting, the conversation could go like this:

"Honey, you know how your friend Katie has a little sister?"

"Yes."

"Well, guess what?"

"What?"

"Remember how we went all the way to China to get you, because we love you and wanted you to be part of our family?"

"Yes."

"Well, remember all the pictures we've seen of other babies from China?"

"The babies without mommies or daddies?"

"Yes, those very special babies. Well, guess what?"

"What, Mommy?"

"You and Daddy and Mommy are going to go to China again! And we're going to come home with a new baby who will be your sister. She'll be oh, so tiny, just as you were. And you'll get to hold her. We'll all love her, just as much as we love you and wanted you to be part of our family. In fact, in a little while, we'll get a picture of her—just like the one we got of you!"

"Will you still love me, Mommy?"

"Honey, we will always love you—just as we always have. You're our precious girl."

What I want you to focus on here is describing a natural part of life without getting into the comparison mistake that we talked about earlier, when we used the example of a husband telling a wife he's going to bring another wife home. Secondly, you need to be very calm. Kids are very intuitive; they can read your emotions and especially your tension as soon as you show the slightest degree of nervousness. If you feel nervous, your firstborn is going to think he should be feeling nervous too. *Maybe this is a bigger deal than Mommy's saying,* he might think.

So make it a fun time, and don't be surprised if you hear things from your firstborn like:

* "Can we give the baby back if we don't like it?"
* "Can we trade her in for a boy if she's a girl?"

ONCE YOU'VE BROKEN THE NEWS

Once you've broken the news, bring your child with you to one of your doctor's appointments. Let her listen to the baby's heartbeat, talk about why Mommy gets weighed and measured, and use this experience as a great natural opportunity to talk about the miracle of birth. If you're adopting, bring your firstborn (if possible and rules allow) to some of your meetings with your agency or the birthmother. Work through paperwork when your firstborn is in the room. If she was also a chosen child, it's a great time to say, "We did all these things for you, too—because we love you. And now we're doing them for your sister."

Four or five months is enough time for a child to adjust if you want to wait that long. You needn't rush this conversation for the sake of your child; remember, the nine months it takes to grow a baby is 25 percent of a three-year-old's life—and in some adoptions, an even higher percentage.

ONCE THE THING IS HOME

Let's go back to our story. Let's say that, despite your protests, your husband actually brought the redhead home. Imagine his conversation as he doted on her:

"Oh, look honey, at her little toes, and her feet! And see how she wears these adorable earrings, and she's so petite! She doesn't have those pudgy knees that you had at her age, and look—no crow's feet around her eyes! Remember when you didn't have any crow's feet? Oh, don't you just love her? Don't you just want to gobble her up?" And then he starts kissing her face all over.

Once again, this is exactly what happens to so many firstborns. Baby is brought into the house, and everybody is looking at the infant. Mom is gushing about her hair, her toes, her fingers, and worse, even comparing everything to the firstborn: "Boy, her cheeks aren't as chubby as Megan's were. Remember Megan's chubby cheeks?"

By now Megan's thinking something's wrong with her, and then she has to watch while her delighted mother kisses baby's toes, face, and tummy—just like she used to kiss Megan's toes, face, and tummy.

Your baby, receiving all that attention, doesn't have a clue about what's going on, but your firstborn, the one being neglected, has never been more aware of her surroundings. And that's something you need to be very aware of before you bring child number two home. It helps if husbands and wives (or, in the case of single parents, the parent and a grandparent or good friend) can "tag team"—showing attention to the firstborn to ease her into this transition. It's also a great idea to give the firstborn a present since baby will probably receive many presents as well.

Expect some hesitancy and wild questions. I've heard toddler-age siblings actually ask, "Are we *really* going to keep it?" with a horrified look on their faces. Once again you have to work hard to keep getting behind your firstborn's eyes. This is a major adjustment in her life, so please don't ask her to just accept it without you taking the time to explain things.

One of the best things you can do, for now and the future, is to undercut arguments about fairness and everybody being treated the same. It is very important that kids learn early on that everyone will not be treated the same. This is the cause of half the fights that siblings get into—from Cain and Abel to the Smothers Brothers. Your job as a parent is to explain why kids can't and won't be treated the same.

219

> "Honey, I'm going to treat you differently because little Annika is just a baby and you're not a baby; you're a big girl [or boy]. You get to stay up until 8:30, but Annika has to go to bed at 7:30. Baby can't watch television either, can she?"
> "No."

"Can she play games with Mommy?"

"No."

"No, she can't. Can we feed the baby popcorn?"

"Nooooo."

"That's right. Babies can't eat popcorn."

This mom is building a case that the firstborn toddler is still special, and that the two children need to be treated differently. With greater maturity come greater privileges and greater responsibility.

Be dramatic! Hold up both hands and say, "Honey, can you count the number of naps a baby has to take in one day? Count with me: one, two, three, four, five, six, seven. That's right. Baby has to take seven naps a day, but you're a big girl. How many naps do you take?"

It's also easier if child number two is a different gender than child number one. Children of different genders may not struggle so much for the firstborn role, and in fact both may develop some firstborn tendencies, even though their personalities will still usually be quite different (one introspective and one very outgoing, for instance).

The whole emotional crux of this process lies in the parent demonstrating, talking, and showing the firstborn that each member of the family gets treated differently. This is easy to do with a three- to four-year gap. It's much more difficult if the gap is eighteen months or less—especially if, as she starts to grow, child number two ends up being bigger or smarter.

Involve the firstborn in daily caring for the baby. She can run and get you a clean diaper or a teething toy. She can learn where the bibs are. With a little guidance, a three-year-old can even sprinkle powder on baby's bottom, but don't turn her loose, unless you want baby to resemble Casper the Friendly Ghost.

TWO BABIES

I'm not talking about twins (though if you have twins, bless you for your double measure of exhaustion!) when I mention that you may find you soon have two babies on your hands. Firstborns, particularly the younger ones, may regress in their development soon after the arrival of child number two. Don't be surprised if this happens in your house.

A girl who may have been potty trained will suddenly start having accidents on a daily basis. A boy who hasn't touched his pacifier in nine months may suddenly be begging you for it—and you're scrambling through old drawers, trying to find that stupid binkie. A child who has been weaned and is eating solid foods may ask you if she can breast-feed once again.

This is normal behavior. Not every child goes through it, but since a good half of all children show some signs of regression, we psychologists view this as a normal rite of passage that firstborns use to cope with the stress of having a sibling. No matter what you do, you physically can't give child number one the same amount of attention you did before you brought child number two home. You've run the great race once again and you have an infant to take care of.

So give a little here; your child is trying to cope. If your two- or even three-year-old wants to nurse again, let her— she'll probably do it just once. If he wants his binkie, get him his binkie. This is a stressful time, so you need to bend with your child.

The regressive behaviors that are most troubling are the attention-getting kind. Just when you need his help the most, your firstborn might go out of his way to make you pay attention to him. He'll make a mess in the bathroom, go fishing in the aquarium, get into the snack cupboard and leave cookie crumbs all over, try to throw the cat in the swimming pool, etc. You'll be amazed at how creative your firstborn can be in getting your attention.

Since the new baby is so helpless, your firstborn will soon learn that the best way to get attention is to create an emergency. Otherwise he knows he'll hear, "Oh, honey, wait just a minute until I put baby down for a nap." Firstborn Franny knows that if she can create a life-threatening situation to herself or the family pet, you'll put the baby down and come running.

If an older child tries to take out her stress on the baby— actually hitting or biting the baby, know this: Firstborn Franny is suffering from an acute case of dethronement. She thinks Mommy doesn't have enough kisses or hugs left over for her. This can usually be solved indirectly, with a simple reassurance that Mommy will always have enough kisses, that Mommy's love couldn't be any greater than it is.

When there's a case of actual hitting or biting, remove the firstborn from the scene and send him to a time-out area. With a stern look, tell him that Mommy isn't happy with him. After the inevitable tears and reassuring hugs, repeat the affirmations that we just talked about. You need to understand the psychology of what's going on: When you remove a child from the scene, you've just isolated him from his Mommy. And guess who's with Mommy? The thing! Firstborn realizes his plan backfired. Instead of driving a wedge between Mommy and the baby, he's driven a wedge between Mommy and himself! That'll get real old, real quick.

It's really important that you talk to your firstborn about his desire for your attention. Have a conversation that goes something like this:

"Honey, everybody likes to get attention. I love it when Daddy kisses me or brings me flowers or hugs me when he comes home. Don't you like it when Daddy gives you a big hug and a kiss when he comes home?"

"Yes."

"Attention is a wonderful thing, isn't it? But you know what? There's another kind of attention people get that isn't so wonderful. Can you guess what that is?"

"Mad attention?"

"Well, sort of. The kind of attention that's negative— when you get yelled at, or screamed at, when you do something naughty and make Mommy or Daddy very angry. That's another kind of attention, but it's negative attention. Do you like that kind of attention?"

"No. Not so much."

"What are some of the things kids do to get negative attention?"

"Hit the baby."

"Yes, that's one."

"Pull the dog's tail."

"That's another."

"Flush the fish."

"That would get negative attention too, wouldn't it? Is that the kind of attention you want, the kind that makes Mommy or Daddy angry at you?"

"Not really."

"I didn't think so."

WALK YOUR CHILD THROUGH ACTUAL SCENARIOS

Then continue your conversation, using actual scenarios of things that your child has tried in order to get your attention:

"When you see Mommy burping the baby and you stamp your feet or throw yourself on the floor, you might get my attention, but that's *negative* attention. You see, I have to take care of the baby just like when you were a baby I had to take care of you. I used to nurse you, change your diapers, burp you, and rock you to sleep just like I do for the baby. So sometimes you just have to wait until I'm able to listen to what you need."

Another good strategy is to meet your firstborn's need for attention by inviting him to help you with the baby. Yes, I know you can do it more quickly and thoroughly without his "help," but he needs to be involved.

"Honey, let me show you how a baby burps and how they need help. Here, put this cloth over your shoulder, and now you hold her. Careful! You have to support her head. All right now, let's gently pat baby on the back, just like this. Good!

"Whup! Did you hear that? We got a burp. We got a little bubble. Now we can lay the baby down and she'll go to sleep. Why don't you go pick out a story, and Mommy will read to you as soon as I put baby down?"

I think it's best to ignore initially regressive behavior and not make such a big deal out of it; it's just your firstborn's way of psychologically handling what to him is a very trau-matic time—rather like you losing your temper at the end of a long day. If the behavior continues, however, or if the child is constantly trying to create negative attention, a firm word helps. You need to communicate to your three- or four-year-old, "Hey, wait a minute, you're Mommy's big girl, not a baby girl. You can wait for Mommy while I take care of this dirty diaper."

If the firstborn won't let up, it's time to apply discipline—a time-out chair or putting him in another room is the most appropriate for this age. My favorite is picking up the child and removing him from the scene. If he won't let you feed or clean the baby, take him to his room and close his door. Tell him, "If you won't let Mommy do what she needs to do, you can't be around Mommy right now. I'll come back and get you when I'm free." As soon as your child realizes that acting up creates less attention and even, on occasion, solitary confinement, much of that regressive behavior will stop. Initially, he may scream his head off, but remember, it's okay to have a kid unhappy with you now and then.

225
· · · · ·

ONE IS THE LONELIEST NUMBER

I can hear some of you thinking right now: *Why bother with having two or more children if the arrival of a new baby is such a traumatic event for the firstborn? In previous generations, you didn't see too many families with just one child, but it's becoming more and more common today.*

Perhaps the best reason I can give you to have more than one child comes from something I've never heard an only child tell me—and I've talked to quite a few in my lifetime. The one thing I've never heard an only child say to me as an adult is, "I want to have an only child." They all want to have more than one child.

Brothers and sisters are sort of like chemotherapy—you don't like them much initially, but ultimately, you really do need them. Having siblings teaches any number of valuable lessons. Children get on-the-job training in terms of sharing. They quickly discover that they are not the center of the universe (something an "only born" may struggle with his entire life). Living with a member of the opposite sex prepares them for marriage by teaching them to relate to members of the other gender. Multiple children have to learn how to cooperate, and they learn to play with someone who isn't their own age.

Every birth order has its advantage. The secondborn benefits from having a trailblazer above her. The firstborn always ends up being a guinea pig and the "practice child." Even after reading this book, you will still overdo it with the firstborn; with the second, you'll lighten up and realize that dirt is not lethal. The firstborn gets a convenient person to blame whenever anything gets broken or winds up missing. The baby of the family gets lots of attention and plenty of people to serve him. Middles get to enjoy less pressure and less attention, and they can develop at their own rate.

Though having a large family isn't a politically correct thing to do in this day and age, I think there's a real blessing in considering it. I've never met someone from a large family who told me they didn't enjoy growing up with multiple siblings. Sure, they admit that it was tough sometimes. There may not have been a lot of money, everybody but the firstborn may have had to wear hand-me-downs, and they rarely got to spend time with Mom or Dad just by themselves, but the joys of having many brothers and sisters outweighed the scarcity of things. In large families, you learn to cooperate, to depend upon each other. You experience the joy of teamwork and sharing, and you learn the very valuable lesson that everybody needs to pitch in and help for the common good.

Another value of large families is that it limits the amount of activities your kids can participate in. Parents are so crazy these days, signing their children up for three or four activities a season, but you can't do that with five, six, or seven children. Money and time just won't permit it. I think this is a blessing, because kids need downtime at home, not busy time on the road.

I appeared on a show with Geraldo Rivera many years ago, and Geraldo interviewed families with 19, 13, 11, and 9 kids. Everyone talked of the joy of having such a large family. One thing that struck me was how mature the younger kids were, while at the same time being pretty naïve about most little-kid stuff. For example, I talked to the youngest child of a large family. He was only four years old, but if a plane flew overhead, he could tell you what kind of plane it was. If you showed him a picture of the Beatles, he knew which one was Paul and which one was John.

Then I tried a little experiment. "Jason," I said, "can you finish this statement: 'Jack and Jill went up a —'"?

Jason gave me a blank look.

"Mary had a little—?"

Jason didn't have a clue.

A firstborn would know all that stuff, but a lastborn in a large family often skips many of the nursery rhymes. This shows you how your own parenting will change with later kids.

The kids with larger families freely admitted that there were difficult times, and the parents confessed that they had those nights when they looked up at the ceiling and asked each other, "How in the world are we going to make it?"

But tell me, what couple hasn't said that at least once in their life? Parents with just one child are bound to think that at some point, too.

In a day when the average family has 1.9 children, I realize that talking about large families is contrarian at best and will seem weird at worst. Some may say to me, "Are you crazy? Don't you know how much it costs to raise a family today?" Yes, I do. Sande and I have five children between the ages of ten and thirty. We know what we're talking about. There are minuses, but the pluses outweigh them big-time; I hope you'll at least consider some of the blessings of raising a larger family.

PAVING THE WAY

To sum things up—yes, it's going to be a bit traumatic for your firstborn when you bring "the thing" home. You can help alleviate this discomfort by carefully considering how you tell your firstborn about the impending birth or adoption, thoughtfully keeping him in mind when you first bring the baby home, and including him in the baby's initial care.

You won't be able to entirely remove your firstborn's anxiety, but that's okay, as I believe that some tension and some unhappiness is good for kids. It's a healthy thing for them to learn how to deal with trials. Because of this, I'm a big advocate of larger families. Siblings really do help us to mature and develop. Bringing another child home may be a "gift" that your firstborn wishes she could take back, but it ultimately will pay big dividends in her future.

EPILOGUE

There's Nothing Better Than Being Loved

Raising a firstborn—or any child—is certainly an awful lot of work. Any parent would admit that. But parenting is also an exciting adventure, full of twists and turns, laughs (yes, some tears too), and surprises. Is it worth it? As the parents of five children, Sande and I would say a resounding "Yes!" Does it mean we aren't ever tired? Certainly not. At times we're bone-weary from all the demands on our time and energies. Are there nights when we roll our eyes at each other and say, "Why us? What did we ever do to deserve this?" Certainly.

But we got into the game—and we stay in the game—because we believe in the power of parenting. So let me close with a true story that reveals the kind of power you have as a parent—not only on your firstborn but on all the children you raise—and on subsequent generations.

Even if you're not a golf fan (and I'm not one myself, particularly), I think you'll be able to relate to this emotional story as a parent.

The U.S. Open is widely considered to have the most brutal playing conditions of any tournament in professional golf. It is also one of four "majors," the most prestigious tournaments on which careers are made or broken.

One of the players participating in the 1998 tournament was Lee Janzen, who hadn't won a golf tournament in three years. In his prior five efforts at the Open, he missed the cut four times (the field gets split in half two days into the tournament; if your scores are in the bottom half, you go home without a paycheck) and won the tournament once, for a schizophrenic record of Cut-Cut-Cut-Win-Cut.

On Saturday night of the 1998 tournament, it certainly didn't look like Janzen's streak of three years without a win would end. He was five strokes behind the leader, and on a course like the U.S. Open, he'd need to play nearly perfect golf and hope that the leaders came back to him. Every reporter pretty much accepted it as gospel truth that if Payne Stewart, on top of the leader board, could shoot even par on Sunday, he'd walk away with the championship.

Janzen didn't help his cause by starting his final round with par-bogie-bogie, putting him seven strokes behind Payne Stewart with fifteen holes to play. He picked up a stroke with a birdie on the next hole, but on the fifth hole, his drive sailed disastrously right, landing in a giant cyprus tree. The trees at this course are very thick, and in one of the worst strokes of luck, Janzen's ball stayed lodged in the branches. He and his caddie searched frantically for the ball, but a fan confirmed it had never come down.

Dejected, certain he had lost the tournament, Janzen started walking back toward the tee, knowing that with the penalty he was looking at a double bogie and falling eight strokes behind Stewart, all but sealing his fate.

Interestingly enough, the U.S. Open always ends on Father's Day (unless there's a Monday playoff), and Janzen was just about to get a present. As he turned his back, some fans excitedly called out. The ball had finally fallen through!

After a couple of great shots, instead of double-bogie, Janzen scored a birdie—and the match was on.

As Stewart faltered, Janzen remained steady. In the end Stewart lost the tournament by leaving a putt six inches wide on the eighteenth hole. Janzen's record was now Cut-Cut-Cut-Win-Cut-Win.

It's exhilarating to win any tournament after a three-year drought, but to end a long losing streak by winning a major has to be about the best feeling there is in golf. But it certainly wasn't the best feeling of Janzen's day. The best was yet to come.

At the press conference, a little four-year-old boy created more than a little commotion. He had been with his baby-sitter all day long, and there wasn't a herd of horses that could pull him away from his dad any longer. Running into his father's arms, Connor Janzen yelled out, "Dad! I missed you. Happy Father's Day!"

How do you think that father felt? In front of a worldwide audience, Lee Janzen couldn't hide the tears. Yeah, it was special winning the U.S. Open—but life has better things in store than even elite vocational success.

"There's nothing better than being loved," he said.[8]

And he's right.

Yes, I've asked you to make sacrifices. There will be times when you won't know where you'll get the money, the emotional energy, or the time you need to invest anything more in your children. But when you dig down deep, you'll amazingly find it. You'll "soar on wings like eagles"; you'll "run and not grow weary"; you'll "walk and not be faint."[9]

And when you do, you'll come across those rare moments like Lee Janzen experienced at the U.S. Open, where even the highest success won't compare to the thrill of having your little boy or your little girl come running into your arms, crying out, "I love you! Happy Mother's Day!"

There really *is* nothing better than being loved—especially by a child.

FAVORITE BABY GAMES

For some "mom and baby" fun time, try these seven classic games that are guaranteed to make baby laugh and you, too. And then invent your own!*

Itsy Bitsy Spider

You've all probably heard of this one:

The itsy bitsy spider went up the water spout,
Down came the rain and flushed the spider out;
Out came the sun and dried up all the rain
And the itsy bitsy spider went up the spout again.

While singing this song, walk your fingers up from your baby's toes toward her chest. When the spider gets flushed out, use both hands and glide them down baby's body—she'll love that. When you say, "Out came the sun," throw your hands widely away from each other in melodramatic fashion, and just watch your baby's eyes grow wide (you should make your own eyes grow wide, too). Then start "walking" up baby's body again.

Games like this combine three things that babies love most: eye contact, touching, and singing.

*Since nursery rhymes are part of a very fluid oral tradition, these versions may vary from other published sources or ones you already use with your family.

Little Bunny Foo Foo

This song works best with vigorous hand motions and melodramatic voicing.

> Little Bunny Foo Foo, hopping through the forest (make rabbit ears with your hands, or put two fingers together from one hand and make them "hop" on your other hand)
> Scooping up the field mice and bopping them on the head (gently pat baby on the head).
> Down came the good fairy and she said, (shake your finger and use a forceful, funny voice, like you're giving a big, melodramatic lecture)
> "Little Bunny Foo Foo, I don't want to see you scooping up the field mice
> And bopping them on the head.
> I gave you three chances and you didn't behave.
> Now you're a goon!
> POOF!

Patty-cake

Yeah, you know this one too.

> Patty-cake, patty-cake, baker's man,
> Bake me a cake as fast as you can.
> Put it in the oven and what do you see?
> Out comes a cake for baby and me.

Once again, the key here is to make hand movements go with the words. Pat baby's hands or feet together as you are making the cake; speed up your motions when you get to "as fast as you can." With the words "for baby and me," point to baby and then point to you.

Five Little Monkeys

This is a great song for naptime.

> *Five little monkeys jumping on the bed.*
> *One fell off and bumped his head*
> *So Momma called the doctor and the doctor said,*
> *"No more monkeys jumping on the bed!"*
>
> *Four little monkeys jumping on the bed.*
> *One fell off and bumped his head*
> *So Momma called the doctor and the doctor said,*
> *"No more monkeys jumping on the bed!"*
>
> *Three little monkeys jumping on the bed.*
> *One fell off and bumped his head*
> *So Momma called the doctor and the doctor said,*
> *"No more monkeys jumping on the bed!"*

235
• • • • •

Then two little, and then one little . . .

> *No little monkeys jumping on the bed.*
> *None fell off and bumped his head*
> *So Momma called the doctor and the doctor said,*
> *"Put those monkeys back in bed!"*

Davy, Davy Dumpling

This is an old one that might make modern parents nervous, but hey, your child has no context to think of anything gruesome and it's a fun rhyme; with the right hand motions, you'll really get baby laughing.

> *Davy, Davy Dumpling,*
> *Boil him in a pot.*
> *Sugar him*
> *Butter him*
> *And eat him while he's hot!*

With the "Davy, Davy Dumpling" line, I like to tickle baby's stomach. When I get to "boil him in a pot," I'll run my hands down both of baby's cheeks. "Sugar him"—this is where you get to gently tickle your baby's tummy. For "butter him," run your hands down baby's legs. And for "eat him while he's hot," you get to give baby a loud, messy raspberry, right on his tummy.

Criss, Cross, Applesauce

For this one, have your baby lie on her stomach.

> *Criss, cross,*
> *Applesauce;*
> *Spiders climbing up your back.*
> *A cool breeze,*
> *A tight squeeze,*
> *Now you've got the shiveries!*

For "criss, cross," make an X along your baby's back with your fingers; for "applesauce," rub the X off. When you get to "spiders climbing," turn your fingers into arachnids, and walk your way up baby's back. "A cool breeze" means you get to gently blow on baby's neck; "a tight squeeze" is exactly what you do to her legs. "Now you've got the shiveries" is the fun part—you get to tickle baby all over! Don't you just love hearing her laugh?

Cobbler, Cobbler

For this one, baby turns over onto her back. It's a feet game, so you want to get real close and let her see your face.

> *Cobbler, cobbler, mend my shoe,*
> *Have it done by half-past two.*

Stitch it up and stitch it down;
Now nail the heel all around.

For the first line, take each foot in one hand and gently pat them together in time with the cadence of your rhyming. When you get to "have it done . . ." switch to baby's toes and wiggle those little digits all around. For "stitch it up," put your thumb and forefinger together and "sew" your baby's foot. The last line, "Now nail the heel," thunk baby's heel very gently with your forefinger.

NOTES

1. Cited in *Steve Martin: The Magic Years* by Morris Walker (New York: S.P.I. books, 2001), 1.
2. Psalm 139:14.
3. Based on a story by S. L. Price, "A Clean Start," *Sports Illustrated,* 28 January 2002, 58ff.
4. "Families and the Labor Market, 1969–1999: Analyzing the 'Time Crunch,'" A Report by the Council of Economic Advisors, May 1999, 13; and Robert Putnam and Christine Goss, "It's About Time," *The San Francisco Chronicle*, 24 September 2000; both cited in Brian Robertson, "Why Daycare Subsidies Do Not Help Parents or Kids," published by the Family Research Council.
5. Associated Press, "Study: Child's Skills Slowed If Mom Returns to Work Early," 18 July 2002.
6. See Ephesians 6:1-3 for a commandment to parents—and a wonderful promise.
7. Cited in Carolyn Jabs, "How to Raise a Sexually Healthy Child," *Redbook*, June 2001, 168.
8. Based on the account provided in *The Majors* by John Feinstein (New York: Back Bay Books, 2000), 318.
9. Isaiah 40:31.

DR. KEVIN LEMAN'S "A CHILD'S TEN COMMANDMENTS TO PARENTS"

1. My hands are small; please don't expect perfection whenever I make a bed, draw a picture, or throw a ball. My legs are short; please slow down so I can keep up with you.

2. My eyes have not seen the world as yours have; please let me explore safely; don't restrict me unnecessarily.

3. Housework will always be there. I'm only little for such a short time—please take time to explain things to me about this wonderful world, and do so willingly.

4. My feelings are tender; please be sensitive to my needs; don't nag me all day long. (You wouldn't want to be nagged for your inquisitiveness.) Treat me as you would like to be treated.

5. I am a special gift from God; please treasure me as God intended you to do, holding me accountable for my actions, giving me guidelines to live by, and disciplining me in a loving manner.

6. I need your encouragement, but not your praise, to grow. Please go easy on the criticism; remember, you can criticize *the things* I do without criticizing *me*.

7. Please give me the freedom to make decisions concerning myself. Permit me to fail, so I can learn from my mistakes.

8. Please don't do things over for me. Somehow that makes me feel that my efforts didn't quite measure up to your expectations. I know it's hard, but please don't compare me with my brother or my sister.

9. Please don't be afraid to leave for a weekend together. Kids need vacations from parents, just as parents need vacations from kids. Besides, it's a great way to show us kids that your marriage is special.

10. Please take me to Sunday school and church regularly, setting a good example for me to follow. I enjoy learning more about God.